Kingfisher Science Encyclopedia

General Editor: Catherine Headlam

6

LEONARDO DA VINCI ● MUSCLE

Kingfisher

KINGFISHER
an imprint of Larousse plc
Elsley House, 24–30 Great Titchfield Street
London W1P 7AD

First published by Kingfisher 1991
Reprinted 1993, 1995 (with revisions) (twice), 1997

British Library Cataloguing-in-Publication Data
A catalogue record for this book is available from the British Library

ISBN 1 85697 452 9

Typesetting: Tradespools Ltd, Frome,
Somerset
Printed in Spain

SAFETY CODE

Some science experiments can be dangerous. Ask an adult to help you with difficult hammering or cutting and any experiments that involve flames, hot liquids or chemicals. Do not forget to put out any flames and turn off the heat when you have finished. Good scientists avoid accidents.

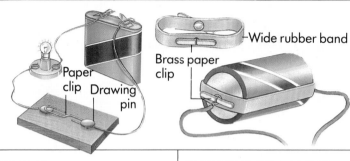

ELECTRICITY
- Never use mains electricity for experiments.
- Use batteries for all experiments that need electricity. Dispose of batteries carefully when they are used up and never heat them up or take them apart.

HEATING
- Tie back hair and be careful of loose clothes.
- Only heat small quantities of a substance.
- Always have an adult with you.
- Never heat any container with a top on it. Always point what you are heating away from you.
- Never hold something in your hands to heat it. Use a holder that does not conduct heat.

SAFE SOURCES OF HEAT
- Hot water from the tap or kettle is a good source of heat.
- A hair dryer can be used to dry things. Always take care when using electricity near water.

SAFE CONTAINERS
- For direct heat use a night light or short thick candle placed in sand in a metal tray.

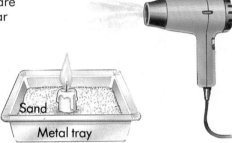

CHEMICALS AND QUANTITIES
- Only use a small amount of any substance even if it is just salt or vinegar.
- Never taste or eat chemicals
- Clean up all spillages immediately, especially if on your skin.
- Wash your hands after using chemicals.
- Always ask an adult before using any substance; many cooking or cleaning substances used at home are quite powerful.
- Smell chemicals very carefully. Do not breathe in deeply any strong smells.
- Never handle chemicals with your bare hands. Use an old spoon and wash it very carefully after use.
- Label **all** chemicals.

SUN
- Never look directly at the Sun, especially when using a telescope or binoculars.

PLANTS AND ANIMALS
- Never pick wild flowers.
- Collect insects carefully so as not to harm them. Release them afterwards.
- Be careful of stinging insects.

SAFE CONTAINERS
- Use plastic containers if an experiment does not require heating or strong chemicals.
- Use heat-proof glass or metal containers if you are using heat.
- Avoid using ordinary glass as it may shatter.

CUTTING
- Use scissors rather than a knife whenever possible.
- When using a knife keep your fingers behind the cutting edge.
- Put what you are cutting on a board that will not slip and will prevent damage to the surface underneath.

Leonardo da Vinci

Leonardo da Vinci (1452–1519) was a great Italian painter, sculptor, architect and engineer who contributed more to science, TECHNOLOGY and art than anyone else of his time. Many of his ideas were hundreds of years ahead of their time. For example, his drawings included plans for a helicopter long before the MATERIALS and technology were available to build one. He was trained as an artist by the painter and sculptor Andrea del Verrocchio. While learning to draw things, he became interested in how they worked. His great paintings include *The Last Supper* and *Mona Lisa*. In 1513 Leonardo was invited to France by the French king, Francis I. He spent his last years living in a castle given to him by the king in Cloux, near Amboise. Many of Leonardo's sketch books are preserved in museums.

▲ Leonardo da Vinci was an artist and an inventor. He also made important discoveries about the structure of the human body.

Lever

A lever transmits a FORCE from one place to another. If you have used a nutcracker, punched a hole with a can opener, or prised up a rock with a stick, you have used a lever. The simplest lever is a rigid bar which is free to twist about a point called the fulcrum. To lift a heavy rock you place a small rock close to the heavy one and then push a bar over the small rock and under the heavy one. The small rock is the fulcrum. By pressing down on the lever (the effort), you will lift the heavy rock. But you have to push the lever down a long way to lift the

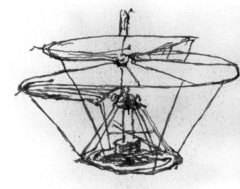

▲ Leonardo sketched this helicopter-like flying machine in the early 1500s. There was no engine shown and this machine did not fly.

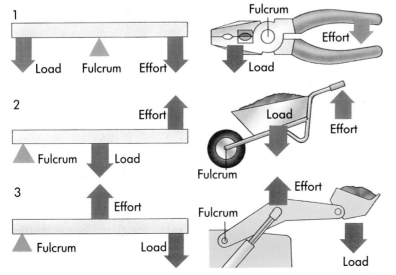

◄ There are three different classes of levers. In a first-class lever **1**, as used in a pair of pliers, the fulcrum is between the load and the effort. A wheelbarrow is an example of a second-class lever **2**, with the load between the fulcrum and the effort. A third-class lever **3**, which is used in a mechanical digger, has the effort between the fulcrum and the load.

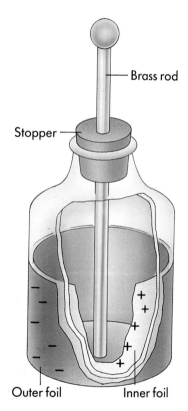

▲ A Leyden jar is a type of capacitor, one of the earliest used to store electric charge. Sheets of foil cover half the jar inside and out. An electric charge applied to the brass rod is stored on the inner foil.

rock a short distance. Using a lever has reduced the effort required but has not reduced the total WORK to be done. By the principle of CONSERVATION of ENERGY, the work done by the effort must equal the work done by the load. The amount of work done is equal to the force multiplied by the distance through which the force moves, so for example, it would be possible to lift a one-tonne car with a force equivalent to the WEIGHT of only 10 kg, if the effort moved through a distance 100 times greater than the load.

Leyden jar

A Leyden jar is used to store ELECTRICITY. It is an early sort of CAPACITOR. It was accidentally discovered by Pieter van Musschenbroek in 1746 at the University of Leiden in The Netherlands. Originally it consisted of a GLASS jar of water with a needle or nail stuck into the water through a cork in the neck of the jar. The glass is an electrical INSULATOR which separates the positive and negative charge. The jar can be charged up by bringing the needle or nail into contact with a charged object; the charge flows down through the needle and the water to the inside edge of the glass.

A more efficient form of jar can be made by coating the inside and the outside of the glass with conducting metal foil and extending the nail or needle down so that it touches the foil on the inside of the jar.

Light

Light is a form of ENERGY that travels freely through space. It is ELECTROMAGNETIC RADIATION just like radio waves, INFRARED RADIATION and X-RAYS. We can see only part of the range of electromagnetic radiation. The part we can see is light. *See* pages 400 and 401.

Light bulb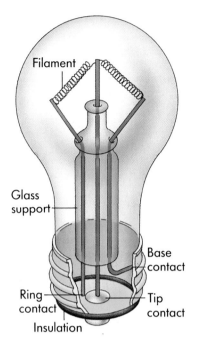

A light bulb is used to produce LIGHT from ELECTRICITY. It consists of a hollow glass ball with a coil of thin wire (the filament) inside. When an electric current flows in the filament, it heats up until it is white hot. In air the filament would burn so bulbs do not have air in them. They are filled with other gases, such as argon, at low pressure in which the filament does not burn.

In other types of bulbs, especially strip lighting, the electric current excites gas molecules in the tube which then emit light. The colour of the light depends on the gas. A sodium vapour bulb, for example, shines yellow. *See also* CIRCUIT, ELECTRIC; LIGHTING, ARTIFICIAL; NEON.

▲ *In a light bulb an electric current flows through a thin coil of wire called a filament. The filament has a high electrical resistance and gets so hot that it glows white and gives off light.*

Light meter

A light meter is an instrument for measuring the amount of LIGHT falling on it. Light on the meter's sensor changes the size of an electric current flowing through it. The change is detected and measured by the meter and shown as a reading of light level on a scale. Light meters are used in PHOTOGRAPHY to ensure that the CAMERA's shutter is open for long enough for the correct amount of light to fall on the film. Modern cameras have built-in light meters. Light meters may also be used to regulate sun-shields in greenhouses.

▼ *This photographer's light meter uses the light-sensitive metal selenium as the sensor in a photoelectric cell. When light shines on the selenium, its electrical resistance decreases because the electrons gain energy from the light and so carry current from a battery through the cell more easily and registers on a galvanometer's scale.*

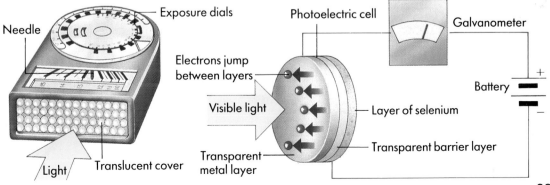

LIGHT

The waves of electromagnetic radiation which make up light do not involve the movement of any material such as air. This means that light can travel even in a vacuum where there is no material of any kind. (Sound waves are a different kind of wave which involve the movement of air and so cannot travel in a vacuum.) Light waves, like other electromagnetic waves, are made up of particles of energy called photons. This energy can be absorbed and also reflected.

Most of the light we see comes originally from very hot objects. The hotter the object, the further towards the blue end of the spectrum is the light that it gives out. (A piece of iron heated in a fire becomes red-hot, then yellow and finally it glows white-hot.) The surface of the Sun, which is heated by the nuclear fusion going on inside, is at a temperature of about 6000°C and it gives out the sunlight which we see.

In empty space, light travels at about 300 million metres per second! The light from the Sun takes 8 minutes to reach the Earth. In 1890 two American scientists, Michelson and Morley found that even though the Earth is moving very quickly around the Sun, the speed of light does not seem to change. This is quite different from what would happen in the case of, for example, sound or water waves if they were coming from the Sun. The theory of relativity explains this as well as why nothing can travel faster than light.

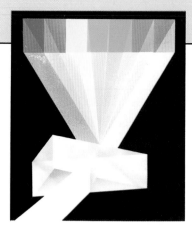

▲ White light passed through a prism bends at the boundary between the air and glass. Each colour that makes up white light has a different wavelength, the red waves bend the least and the violet the most. The white light splits up into its component waves and shows the spectrum of colours known as the visible spectrum.

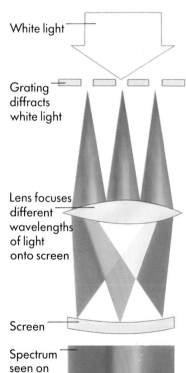

White light

Grating diffracts white light

Lens focuses different wavelengths of light onto screen

Screen

Spectrum seen on screen

▲ White light can also be split into a spectrum by the process of diffraction because the different wavelengths (colours) are diffracted different amounts. The light is passed through the very narrow slits of a diffraction grating.

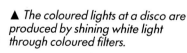

▲ The coloured lights at a disco are produced by shining white light through coloured filters.

◄ Objects look a certain colour because they reflect part of the spectrum and absorb the rest. The leaves of plants appear green because they do not absorb the green part of the spectrum.

Glass   Plastic   Cardboard

▲ Light travels through glass well, so objects can be clearly seen through it. Substances which allow light to pass well are called transparent. Some plastics absorb a small amount of light, they are translucent. Cardboard allows no light to pass through, it is opaque.

▼ Objects lit by a bright source of light cast shadows. These Indonesian shadow puppets cast shadows on a wall or a translucent screen and are used to illustrate stories.

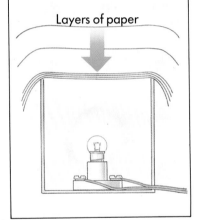

SEE FOR YOURSELF
You can test the translucency of various materials, such as sheets of paper, using a torch bulb in a cardboard box. Put sheets of paper onto the open top of the box one sheet at a time, and see how the layers become less translucent as the sheets are added.

Layers of paper

Christiaan Huygens (1629–1695)
Huygens was a Dutch physicist and mathematician who first suggested that light travels as waves. He explained reflection and refraction in terms of wave motion. He invented new ways of making glass lenses for telescopes. With his improved telescope, he was able to see the true shape of the rings around Saturn.

Light has the highest speed of anything known. It travels through the vacuum of empty space at a constant speed of nearly 300,000 kilometres per second. But light slows down when it travels through a material such as glass.

SEE FOR YOURSELF
To make a ray box, take a rectangular cardboard box with a lid and cut a narrow vertical slit in one end. Use strong sticky tape to fix a lamp holder wired to a battery inside the box. You can use the ray of light that comes out of the slit to see how an angled mirror reflects light round corners. You will be able to see the light ray more clearly in a darkened room.

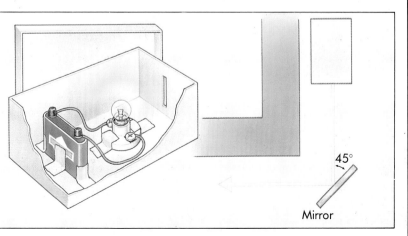

45°

Mirror

See also COLOUR; ELECTROMAGNETIC RADIATION; ENERGY; LENS; MIRROR; PHYSICS; PRISM; SPECTRUM; SUN; VACUUM; WAVELENGTH; WAVES.

Thomas Edison not only invented the first successful electric lamp, he also invented the first efficient electric generators to supply his lamps with current. In 1882 he began supplying current for more than a thousand of his lamps in the Wall Street district of New York city. Edison's original lamp had a life of about 40 hours, compared to the modern lamp's 1000 hours.

Lighting, artificial

Artificial lighting frees people from the natural cycle of day and night created by the SUN. Most artificial lights work by passing an electric current through a wire or a GAS to make it glow. Glass tubes filled with gases that produce coloured light are used in decorative lighting for shops and advertising. Neon and other NOBLE GASES, such as argon and krypton, are used for this.

Coloured lighting is not suitable for the home or work where white light is needed. Fluorescent lights are gas-filled tubes. A coating of phosphor inside the tube converts invisible ULTRAVIOLET energy produced by the gas into white light. Electric LIGHT BULBS are filled with inert gases at low pressure. These do not react with the hot wire, allowing it to reach a higher temperature and give out more light without burning.

▶ Strip lights give out different coloured lights depending on the particular gas that the tube is filled with. The manufacturers test the tubes they produce and are always looking for ways to improve their efficiency and quality.

▶ A fluorescent lamp, as used in strip lighting, contains mercury vapour at very low pressure. Electric current flowing through an electrode at one end of the tube produces a stream of electrons. These 'excite' mercury atoms, making one of the mercury's electrons move into a higher orbit. When the excited electron jumps back to its normal orbit, the atom gives off invisible ultraviolet light. This hits a phosphor coating on the inside of the tube, making it glow and give off a bright light.

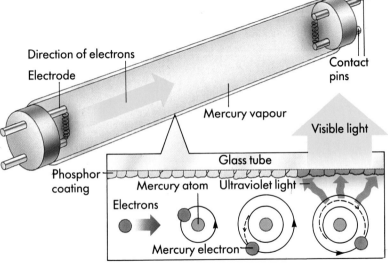

Direction of electrons

Electrode

Contact pins

Mercury vapour

Visible light

Phosphor coating

Glass tube

Mercury atom   Ultraviolet light

Electrons

Mercury electron

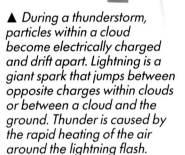

◄ *In a thunderstorm the sky may be filled with dramatic forked lightning.*

Positive charges rise

Negative charges sink

Positive charges rise from ground

▲ *During a thunderstorm, particles within a cloud become electrically charged and drift apart. Lightning is a giant spark that jumps between opposite charges within clouds or between a cloud and the ground. Thunder is caused by the rapid heating of the air around the lightning flash.*

▼ *An experimental lightning conductor on top of a hill.*

Lightning

Lightning may be thought of as a huge spark of ELECTRICITY caused when there is a difference in electrical potential between some part of a thunder CLOUD and the ground, within the thunder cloud itself, or between two clouds. The spark, or electrical discharge, finds the line of least resistance so that it may take on a forked pattern (forked lightning). If the discharge takes place within the cloud, the cloud itself hides the forked pattern and a diffuse glow of LIGHT is seen (sheet lightning). When the lightning discharges its electricity to Earth, it tends to strike at a high point, such as a mountain, a tree, or a tall building.

Lightning flashes produce about 100 million volts of electricity and heat the air to over 33,000°C. It is this rapid heating of the air that causes THUNDER.

Lightning conductor

A LIGHTNING conductor consists of a METAL rod, often on the top of a building connected by a wire or cable to a ground rod buried in the Earth. Lightning tends to strike at high points. In areas where THUNDER storms are common, tall buildings could be damaged by lightning if they are struck. One way to protect such buildings is by means of a lightning conductor. The lightning tends to be attracted to the lightning conductor and is discharged safely to Earth.

The lightning conductor was invented in the mid 18th century by the American statesman and scientist, Benjamin FRANKLIN.

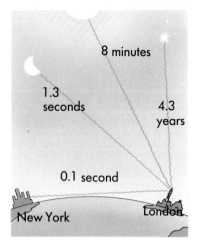

▲ *A light-year is the distance light travels in a year. Light takes 8 minutes to reach Earth from the Sun. Light from the next nearest star takes 4·3 years: the star is 4·3 light-years away.*

▼ *A linear motor train uses magnetic fields to provide it with forward movement. It also uses the repulsion between like magnetic poles to make the train hover over its single rail.*

Light-year

A light-year is the distance a beam of light travels in a year, 9,460,700,000,000 km. Light travels at a speed of 299,792 km/s. Nothing travels faster. Light-years are a useful unit for measuring the huge distances between STARS and GALAXIES. For example, the nearest star after our Sun, PROXIMA CENTAURI, is over four light-years away. Most astronomers prefer to measure distances with the PARSEC, which equals 3.2 light-years.

Linear motor

A linear motor, or linear induction motor, is a type of electric MOTOR. An electric motor is normally made from a series of ELECTROMAGNETS wrapped around a wire coil. When an electric current flows through the coil, magnetic and electric forces between the coil and the electromagnets make the coil spin. If the electromagnets are unrolled and laid flat, a metal bar can be made to skim along their length. This is a linear motor. The first linear motors were made during World War II to help launch aircraft from ships.

Linear motors are being used to propel high-speed trains that do not run on rails. They either float on a cushion of air or are supported by MAGNETS.
See also INDUCTANCE; MAGNETIC LEVITATION.

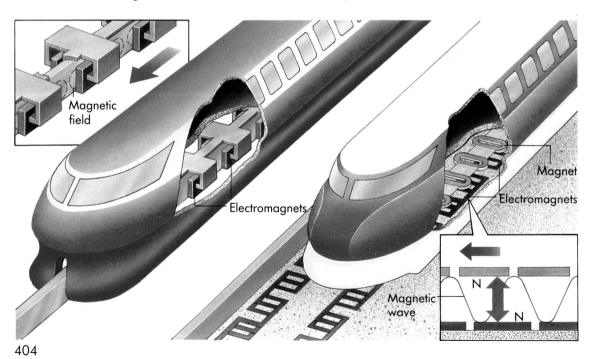

Daisy (*Bellis perennis L.*)

Dog rose(*Rosa canina L.*)

Common Juniper
(*Juniperus communis L.*)

▲ *Linnaeus used his two-word ('binomial') naming system to name many common plants. The first name is the plant's genus; the second, the species.*

Linnaeus, Carolus

Linnaeus (1707–1778) was a Swedish botanist who introduced a standard method of naming and classifying living things. Linnaeus spent much of his childhood collecting plants and animals before studying to become a doctor at the University of Uppsala. In 1741 he was appointed Professor of Medicine and Botany at Uppsala, and so spent more time studying the ECOLOGY and distribution of plants. He described nearly 8000 plant SPECIES and about 4400 animal species (almost everything known to Europeans at the time) and he gave each a scientific name in two parts. For example, he called the wolf *Canis lupus* and the jackal *Canis aureus*. *Canis* is the genus to which the animals belong, and so the scientific name shows that the animals are related.
See also CLASSIFICATION.

▲ *Linnaeus classified animals and plants scientifically.*

Lipids *See* Fats

Lippershey, Hans *See* Telescope

Liquid

A liquid is a STATE OF MATTER in which the ATOMS or MOLECULES are not fixed rigidly in position relative to each other, as they are in a SOLID, but do not move around quite as independently as they do in a GAS. This means that, unlike a solid, a liquid can flow freely and take up any shape but that, unlike a gas, the molecules tend to stick together in drops rather than simply spreading out to fill any container. A liquid is also unlike a gas in that it cannot easily be compressed, or squashed into a smaller

The most common, most useful and in many ways most unusual liquid is water. It fills the world's lakes, rivers and oceans, and falls as rain. It is essential for life – without it, plants and animals soon die. Water dissolves many substances, from salt and sugar to instant coffee. Like all liquids it changes to a solid if it is made cold enough. At below 0°C, water freezes to form ice. But unlike almost every other substance, frozen water expands (takes up more space) as it cools.

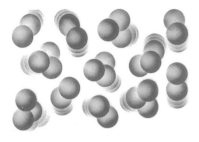

▲ *The molecules in a liquid are free to move around. Like a solid, a liquid has a definite volume but unlike a solid it has no shape of its own; it takes on the shape of the container that holds it.*

volume, by PRESSURE because the FORCES between the molecules prevent them from coming too close together.

Liquids can undergo changes of state to other forms of matter. If they are cooled down, the atoms move around less and FREEZE into fixed positions to form a solid; for example, water freezes to form ice. If liquids are heated, the molecules begin to move so quickly that they evaporate, escaping from the liquid to form a gas. Some substances, such as CARBON DIOXIDE, do not exist as liquids at ordinary pressures and sublime, that is change straight from a solid to a gas. A gas can be liquefied by being cooled. A VAPOUR can be liquefied either by being cooled or by increasing pressure. Bottled gas is liquid butane under pressure which vaporizes when it is released from the pressurized container.
See also EVAPORATION.

When we say liquid, we think of compounds that are liquid at room temperature. Of course many other things can be liquid too. Solid metals melt to become liquids at high temperatures and gases can be cooled to become liquids. Amazingly there are many uses for liquid air. Air becomes liquid at about −190°C and it is used to produce liquid nitrogen and liquid oxygen. Liquid mercury becomes as hard as steel if liquid air is poured over it.

Liquid crystal display (LCD)

A liquid crystal display or LCD is a type of screen used in ELECTRONIC equipment such as digital watches and pocket calculators. It is a sandwich of two sheets of glass with a material called a LIQUID CRYSTAL between them. A thin clear layer of material that conducts ELECTRICITY is on the inside surfaces of the glass. When no current flows between the glass sheets, the liquid crystal is clear. When a current flows between them, crystals in the liquid turn and block the light, turning the display black. If the electrodes on the glass are divided into areas that are controlled separately, the display can show the time, a TELEVISION picture or other shapes.

Liquid crystals were first observed by Friedrich Reinitzer in 1888, but no one could find a use for them. They remained a laboratory curiosity for about 70 years.

▶ *Calculators with liquid crystal displays are familiar objects. Specialist scientific calculators perform lots of different calculations and some even display graphs as well.*

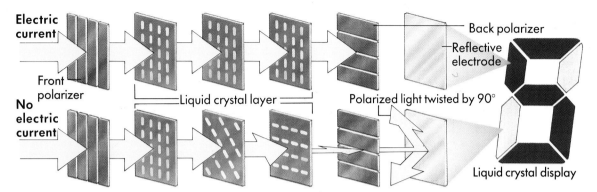

Electric current
Front polarizer
No electric current
Liquid crystal layer
Polarized light twisted by 90°
Back polarizer
Reflective electrode
Liquid crystal display

Liquid crystals

Liquid crystals are materials that flow like water but have a structure like a CRYSTAL. Small changes in electric current or TEMPERATURE can change the way that light passes through the liquid crystal. One type, used in LIQUID CRYSTAL DISPLAYS for calculators and watches, changes from transparent to opaque when an electric current flows through it. Another type, used to make paper-thin flexible thermometers, changes colour when its temperature changes.

▲ *In a liquid crystal display the crystal is between two polarizing filters at right-angles to each other, which together block polarized light. When there is no electric current, light is twisted through 90° by the crystals, so that it passes through the rear polarizer and is reflected back. Applying an electric current straightens the crystals so that the light cannot pass through the rear polarizer. This turns the segment black.*

Lister, Joseph *See* Antiseptics

Litmus

Litmus is a red or blue powder obtained from certain types of plants called lichens. It is a mixture of organic compounds that is prepared by treating the lichen with ammonia, potash and lime. Litmus is SOLUBLE in water or alcohol and is used as a chemical INDICATOR to test whether SOLUTIONS are ACIDS or alkalis. Acids turn blue litmus red and alkalis turn red litmus blue. Litmus paper is absorbent paper impregnated with litmus solution. Most litmus is obtained from lichens that grow in the Netherlands. It was once used as a DYE.

▼ *A liquid crystal display consists of a clear front electrode, etched with a pattern of segments which form numbers. Behind this is a layer of liquid crystal, which is backed up by a reflecting electrode.*

Front, clear electrode
Liquid crystal layer
Back, reflective electrode

Acid

Litmus paper

Acid and litmus solution

Alkali

Alkali and litmus solution

◄ *Litmus is a vegetable dye that turns red in acids and blue in alkalis.*

407

▼ *The liver acts as a chemical factory. One of its jobs is to store and process food materials coming from the digestive system. A blood vessel called the hepatic portal vein carries blood direct from the intestines to the liver. The hepatic artery brings blood directly from the heart to feed the liver itself. The liver also produces a digestive fluid called bile. This collects in the gall bladder and runs down the bile duct to the intestine, where it helps to break down fats. One of the liver's main tasks is to remove any poisons from the blood.*

Liver

The liver is the body's largest GLAND, weighing about 1.5 kg. It is positioned in the abdomen just below the ribs, and is a large, dark red, flattened organ. The liver is unusual in that it has two separate BLOOD supplies. One blood supply provides oxygen and removes waste, just like any other organ. The other blood supply comes directly from the intestine, carrying all the dissolved materials produced by the digestion of food. The liver is made up of thousands of lobules, which are small collections of liver cells surrounded by tiny blood vessels.

The liver processes food for the whole body. At least 500 CHEMICAL REACTIONS take place here. Among the most important is the processing of lipids, which are the result of digesting FAT. One of the products of this process is CHOLESTEROL which is needed by the nervous system and in the production of some HORMONES. The liver breaks down and rebuilds PROTEINS. It also produces urea as a waste product which is later removed by the KIDNEYS; and it converts SUGARS into glycogen, which is stored until needed to power MUSCLES.

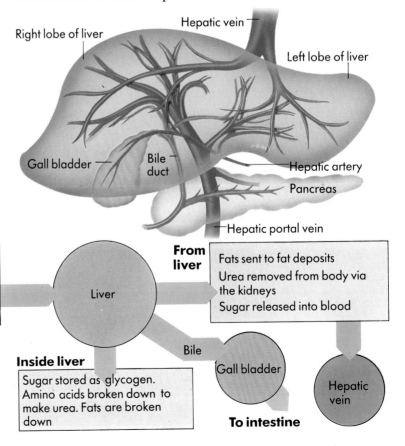

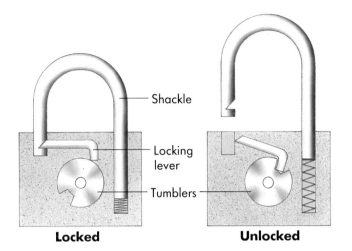

Shackle

Locking lever

Tumblers

Locked   **Unlocked**

◀ *A padlock stays locked because a locking lever engages with a notch in the shackle. Turning the key rotates the tumblers until a slot in the tumblers disengages the locking lever, and a spring pushes up the shackle.*

Locks and Keys

Locks are used to prevent doors, drawers and containers from being opened. When a door is closed, a bolt slides out from the lock into a hole in the door frame, locking the two together. Pins inside the lock fall into place through the bolt and stop it from sliding back. The lock is opened by inserting the correct key in the keyhole to raise the pins and free the bolt. Ancient Egyptians first used locks like this 4000 years ago.

In 1848, Linus Yale invented a modern version of the Egyptian pin lock. The jagged edge of its key raises metal pins or tumblers to the correct height to free the bolt. Most locks that protect outside doors are still Yale-type locks. Some locks are designed to be opened by magnetic keys. Magnets in the key repel the tumblers and free the bolt. Electronic locks work by operating the tumblers when the correct number or word is entered on a keypad. Some locks, especially in banks, are fitted with a timing device which allows the lock to be opened only at certain times. Combination locks are opened by turning a dial to a series of numbers which lines up slots in a series of rings. Electrical switch locks in vehicles need an ignition key. When the key is turned an electric current flows from the BATTERY to the starter motor.

Chemical Keys
The idea that there is a key to every lock has led to the word 'key' being used to mean the answer to a problem. The word is also used when scientists are trying to explain the workings of complex biochemical processes. Catalysts, which help particular reactions but are not used up in them, can be likened to a 'lock' that will only work when the right 'key' molecules fit into them.

▼ *1 A cylinder lock, commonly known as a Yale lock, has a series of spring-loaded pins. The pins are in two parts of unequal lengths. 2 When the key is inserted into the lock, the springs push the pins down into notches in the key. 3 The divisions between the two parts of each pin line up, allowing the cylinder to turn and move the bolt across.*

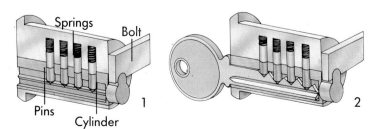

Springs
Bolt
Pins
Cylinder
1

2

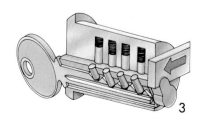

3

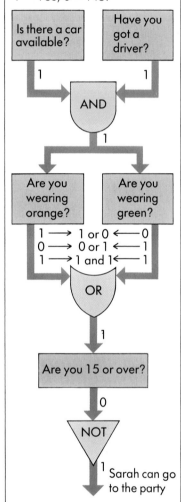

Logic Gates

Sarah is invited to a party 30 km away. It's an orange and green party for under 15 year olds. Can she go? 1 = Yes, 0 = No.

Is there a car available?

Have you got a driver?

1 — 1

AND

1

Are you wearing orange?

Are you wearing green?

1 ⟶ 1 or 0 ⟵ 0
0 ⟶ 0 or 1 ⟵ 1
1 ⟶ 1 and 1 ⟵ 1

OR

1

Are you 15 or over?

0

NOT

1

Sarah can go to the party

Electronic chips used in computers apply the rules of logic. The electrical switches, or logic gates, pass on, or change, the electrical 0s and 1s that go through them. An AND gate needs two 1s for a 1 to come out. An OR gate gives a 1 if either of the two input channels has a 1 going in and a NOT gate reverses the signal so a 0 going in becomes a 1.

Locomotion *See* Movement and Motion

Logic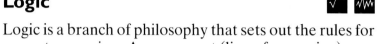

Logic is a branch of philosophy that sets out the rules for correct reasoning. An argument (line of reasoning) consists of a series of statements called premises followed by another statement, called a conclusion. If the conclusion is supported by the premises, then the argument is sound or correct. If the conclusion does not follow from the premises, the argument is unsound. For example, the following argument is sound: all mammals are warm-blooded; all cats are mammals. Therefore all cats are warm-blooded. The following argument is unsound: No dogs are green; some parrots are green. Therefore, some parrots are not dogs. Both premises are true, but the conclusion is not.

The ancient Greek ARISTOTLE developed logic about 300 BC. Today, logic is very important in MATHEMATICS and in COMPUTER programming where statements such as IF X = 1 THEN END are used to tell the computer to finish the program when X equals 1. Computers and other electronic devices contain logic circuits that perform logical operations on two or more input signals.

SEE FOR YOURSELF

Logic is a key tool in any kind of analysis, including that used by a detective. For instance, a detective was called to a hotel following the theft of a diamond ring. Only four people, the cleaner, the maid, the waiter and the porter, had a chance to steal it, and the detective questioned three of them. She then said she knew who the thief was. How could she have found the thief without talking to the fourth suspect? But she had enough information already to know who was guilty. Each of the three suspects had told one truth and one lie.
The cleaner said: "It wasn't me, it was the maid."
The maid said: "It wasn't the cleaner, it was the porter."
The waiter said: "It wasn't the porter, it was the maid."
Can you work out who the thief was?

First of all, you need to make an assumption and then test it. If your assumption produces two statements that contradict each other then your assumption is wrong and you need to make a different assumption. When all the statements agree with your assumption, then your assumption is correct and you too will know who is guilty. For example let's assume that the cleaner told a lie first and the truth second. This cannot be correct because the two statements contradict each other – if 'it wasn't me' is a lie then it was the cleaner, but then 'it was the maid' is true and it can't be, so the assumption that the cleaner told a lie followed by the truth is incorrect.
Answer on p. 412.

Longitude *See* Latitude and Longitude

Loudspeaker

A loudspeaker is a device for changing an electric current into SOUND. The output from a RADIO, TELEVISION or HI-FI system is an electric current changing in step with the sounds that it represents. This is fed to a wire coil inside the loudspeaker. The changing electric current produces a magnetic field that changes in the same way. This changing field repeatedly pulls a MAGNET towards it and then pushes it away again, making the magnet vibrate. The magnet is attached to a paper or plastic cone which vibrates too. These vibrations pass through the air as a stream of pressure waves which our EARS hear as sounds. Most recorded music and many radio and television programmes are now made in STEREO, requiring two loudspeakers.
See also MICROPHONE.

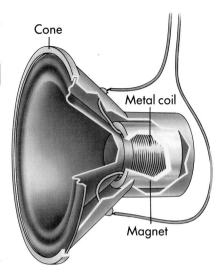

▲ *A loudspeaker has a coil of wire attached to a diaphragm in the shape of a cone. A magnet surrounds the coil. When a sound signal from an amplifier passes through the coil, it moves in step with the signal and makes the cone vibrate, producing sound.*

Lubrication

Lubrication is the use of slippery MATERIALS to make surfaces slide over each other more easily and reduce FRICTION. Without lubrication, surfaces grind against each other and wear down very quickly, shortening the life of a MACHINE or ENGINE. Most lubricants (materials used for lubrication) are liquids made from crude oil, but some are solid. Graphite, also used in pencils, is a solid which can be used as a lubricant. There are also artificial or synthetic lubricants.

Most lubricants become thinner as their temperature

Lubrication is one of the most important techniques in modern industry and engineering. In the engine of a car or lorry, oil is continuously pumped over all the moving parts to prevent them from wearing and getting hot. When a ship is launched, the slipway is greased so that the vessel slides easily down it into the water. In drilling a borehole to underground deposits of oil, engineers pour liquid mud down the hole to lubricate the drill.

Without lubrication

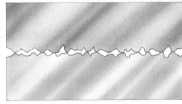

With lubrication

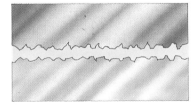

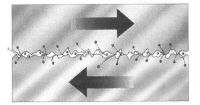

◀ *Seen under a microscope, no surface is perfectly smooth, not even polished metal. When two surfaces move past each other (left), the roughness causes friction. A lubricant holds the surfaces slightly apart (right) so that they slide easily over each other.*

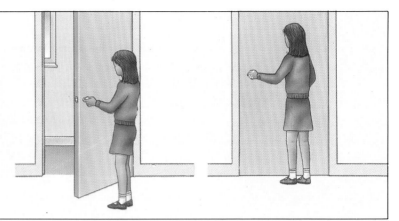

Answer to Logic problem on p. 410:
If you assume that the three first statements were true, you get the following—
Cleaner: "It wasn't me" (true) "It was the maid" (false).
Maid: "It wasn't the cleaner" (true) "It was the porter" (false).
Waiter: "It wasn't the porter" (true) "It was the maid" (false).
From this you can see that the thief was not the cleaner, the maid or the porter, so it had to be the waiter.

rises and thinner lubricants provide less protection to moving parts. Some engines, racing car engines for example, are fitted with oil coolers to keep the oil temperature down and give maximum protection to the engine. Although most vehicle engines have a separate cooling system that uses water and air, the lubrication system can also help to cool the engine.

There are natural lubricants too. Inside joints such as the knee a liquid called synovial fluid lubricates the cartilage caps on the ends of the bones and allows them to slide across each other.

Luminescence

Luminescence is the production of LIGHT by a material, usually a solid. It happens because ELECTRONS in the solid jump from a higher ENERGY to a lower energy; the total amount of energy is conserved, so the extra energy is given out as light. Energy has to be given to the electrons in the material in the first place to make the

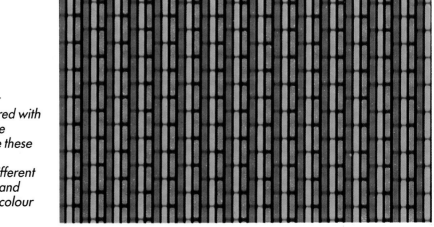

▶ The inside of a colour television screen is covered with phosphor dots. When the beams of electrons strike these dots, they produce luminescence of three different colours. These red, blue and green dots make up the colour pictures we see.

luminescence occur; this can be done in several ways. For example, when the energy comes from light shone onto the material, the luminescence is called *photoluminescence*, and when the energy comes from fast particles colliding with the material, it is called *fluorescence*. Often materials continue to give out light for some time after the input of energy has stopped; this is called *phosphorescence*.

The most common use for luminescence is on the screens of CATHODE RAY TUBES in TELEVISIONS. The screen has phosphor dots on the inside which luminesce when hit by the beam of electrons in the tube, which scans the screen very quickly. Different phosphor dots luminesce at different WAVELENGTHS in colour television.

See also BIOLUMINESCENCE.

Fireflies produce a greenish light known as *bioluminescence*. This heatless light is caused by the effect which two or more chemicals have on each other, and is a much more efficient way of making light than we have yet discovered. There is no waste of energy in the form of heat as in an electric light bulb.

Lungs

Lungs are large rubbery organs positioned in the chest, protected by the ribs. Their function is to take in oxygen needed for respiration, and to pass out waste carbon dioxide and water vapour from the body. Unlike many more primitive animals, all amphibians, reptiles, birds and mammals have lungs to allow them to obtain OXYGEN from the air. Simpler animals, some larval amphib-

▼ The lungs remove carbon dioxide from the blood and replace it with oxygen. The oxygen comes from air breathed in through the trachea. The trachea divides into bronchi and these divide into bronchioles. The bronchioles end as tiny air sacs called alveoli. The pulmonary artery, a great blood vessel from the heart divides into two branches, each going to one of the lungs. Here they divide again and again until they become tiny blood vessels called capillaries. The oxygen breathed into the alveoli passes through the thin alveoli walls and enters the capillaries from the heart. Once this exchange of oxygen for carbon dioxide has taken place, the bright red oxygen-laden blood goes into the pulmonary veins and back to the heart to be pumped around the body.

Trachea

Vena cava

Pulmonary artery

Bronchiole

Alveoli

Aorta

Heart

Pulmonary veins

Bronchi

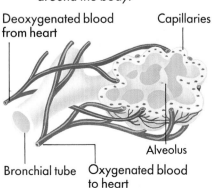

Deoxygenated blood from heart

Capillaries

Bronchial tube

Alveolus

Oxygenated blood to heart

413

▶ *During breathing we do not completely fill and empty our lungs. The lungs always contain about 1500 cm³ (1.5 litres) of air. Normal breathing involves breathing in and out about an extra 500 cm³ (0.5 litres) of air. If we take a deep breath we can increase the air in our lungs by an extra 3000 cm³ (3 litres). If we breathe out hard, we can expel about an extra 1000 cm³. During exercise, the volume of air involved in normal breathing can increase two or three times.*

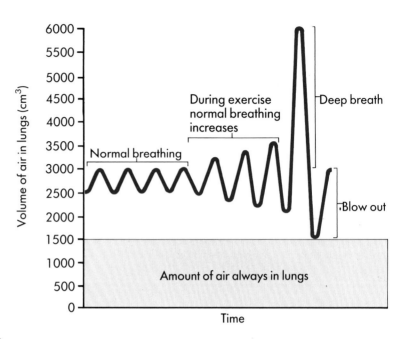

SEE FOR YOURSELF

Take a large plastic bottle (5 litres) and a dish. Put some water in the dish and fill the bottle completely. Then, with your hand over the end of the bottle so that no air gets in, turn it upside down and place it in the dish. (You may need someone to hold the bottle.) A couple of elastic bands and a ruler will make a scale. Place a tube in the end of the bottle. Take a deep breath and then breathe out into the tube. The air from your lungs will fill the bottle and give a measure of your lung capacity.

ians and fish have GILLS or other organs for BREATHING.

In humans, air passes into the lungs along the trachea or windpipe, which splits into smaller bronchi, supplying the air to each lung. The bronchi divide again and again until very small air tubes open into groups of tiny air sacs called alveoli. There are more than 300 million alveoli in the lungs. Oxygen can pass through the thin walls of the alveoli into BLOOD capillaries, while carbon dioxide passes out in the same way. The lungs fill when the muscular diaphragm beneath them contracts and the ribs are raised by the chest muscles. This makes the space inside the chest larger, and the lungs expand to fill the space, drawing air in.

Lyell, Charles *See* Geology

Lymph system

Lymph is a FLUID which leaks from the BLOOD capillaries, and resembles blood without the red cells. It contains many white cells which are used to fight INFECTION, and also contains fat droplets collected from the INTESTINES. Lymph travels through the body along the tubes of the lymph system, and eventually returns to the blood supply near the HEART.

At various points around this lymph system are the lymph glands, which are small swellings containing huge numbers of white blood cells. These white cells in the

The lymph system

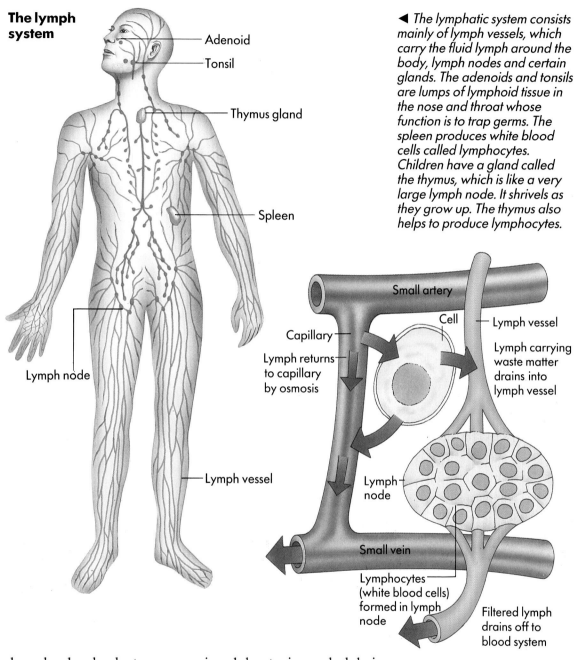

Adenoid

Tonsil

Thymus gland

Spleen

Lymph node

Lymph vessel

Small artery

Cell

Lymph vessel

Capillary

Lymph returns to capillary by osmosis

Lymph carrying waste matter drains into lymph vessel

Lymph node

Small vein

Lymphocytes (white blood cells) formed in lymph node

Filtered lymph drains off to blood system

◄ *The lymphatic system consists mainly of lymph vessels, which carry the fluid lymph around the body, lymph nodes and certain glands. The adenoids and tonsils are lumps of lymphoid tissue in the nose and throat whose function is to trap germs. The spleen produces white blood cells called lymphocytes. Children have a gland called the thymus, which is like a very large lymph node. It shrivels as they grow up. The thymus also helps to produce lymphocytes.*

lymph glands destroy occasional bacteria and debris from dead cells. But when there is an infection, the white cells in the lymph glands multiply very rapidly to fight the intruders. This extra activity causes the lymph glands to become swollen, and it is often a sign of infection when they can be felt in the side of the neck.

White blood cells are made in the lymph nodes of adults and in children in the thymus. The thymus shrinks away in adults but does not disappear.

See also IMMUNE SYSTEM.

▲ *A lymph node is a lump of tissue along a lymph vessel. It forms lymphocytes, which are white blood cells that help to fight infection. It also filters the lymph, carrying waste matter from cells, before it passes into the blood system. Lymph nodes are concentrated in the armpits groin, neck and down the front of the chest.*

Lever

Pulley

Ramp

▲ *Simple machines include levers, pulleys and an inclined plane (above), which give a mechanical advantage for lifting a load. An inclined plane may be used with a wheel and axle in the form of a winch (above right). A wedge (far right) is another simple machine which uses the force of a falling hammer, in this case to split a log.*

416

Mach, Ernst *See* Mach number

Machines, simple

Simple machines are used to help people do things. There are six types of simple machine: the axle, LEVER, PULLEY, SCREW, wedge and wheel. The wheel enables loads to be moved more easily by reducing the FRICTION between the load and the ground. An axle is a shaft that enables wheels to spin round the fixed axle instead of rolling under the vehicle.

A lever is simply a bar supported by a pivot or fulcrum. Pulling one end of the lever down raises the load at the other end. By choosing the position of the fulcrum carefully, a small FORCE on one end of the lever can raise a heavy load at the other end. The wedge, starting from a thin edge and gradually getting thicker, is very useful for separating things. An axe blade is a wedge. A pulley is a wheel with a grooved edge around which a rope or chain fits. Pulleys can change the direction of the force produced by pulling a rope. A number of pulleys can work like a lever by enabling a small force to move a heavy load. Screws are used to fasten things together or to move things.

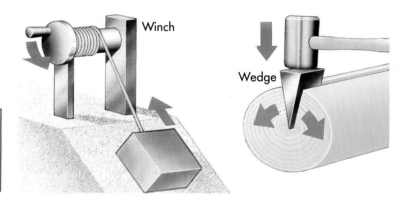
Winch

Wedge

Machine tools

Machine tools are powered tools designed to shape metal, wood and other materials (called a workpiece) by shaving unwanted material off it. There are several ways of doing this. The workpiece can be spun at high speed in a machine tool called a LATHE while cutting tools are pressed into it. Holes can be drilled in it by a drilling machine. Waste material can be cut away by a toothed wheel in a milling machine. It can also be planed in a

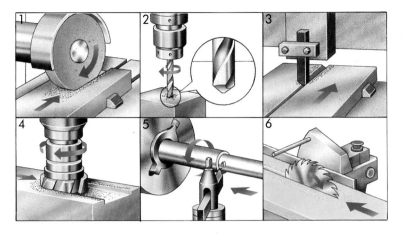

◀ Machine tools include **1** a grinding machine, **2** a drill, **3** a router, **4** a milling machine, **5** a lathe and **6** a circular saw. In all but the drill, the workpiece moves past the cutting tool.

▼ At 1340 miles per hour (about 2150 km/h), Concorde is approaching its top speed of about Mach 2.

planing machine or worn down gradually by a roughened spinning wheel in a grinding machine.

The first machine tools were used during the INDUSTRIAL REVOLUTION when metal parts for STEAM ENGINES and other machines had to be exact so that they would fit any engine or machine. Before then, parts for machines were made by hand for one particular machine.

Mach number

The Mach number is a measurement of speed named after the man who suggested it, Ernst Mach. If the speed of an aircraft is divided by the speed of SOUND in air, the result is the Mach number. Speeds below Mach 1 are called *subsonic*. Speeds above Mach 1 are *supersonic* and speeds above Mach 5 are *hypersonic*. When an aircraft's speed increases beyond Mach 1, it is said to have broken the SOUND BARRIER. All passenger airliners are subsonic except Concorde, which flies at speeds above Mach 2 (twice the speed of sound).

Ernst Mach (1838–1916)
Mach was an Austrian physicist who gave his name to the Mach number. This number is a method of relating an object's speed to the speed of sound in a particular medium, usually air. He also worked on shock waves and inertia, coming to conclusions that conflicted with Einsteins' theory of relativity.

▼ The top speeds of the world's fastest aircraft have increased by more than six times between 1940 and 1990.

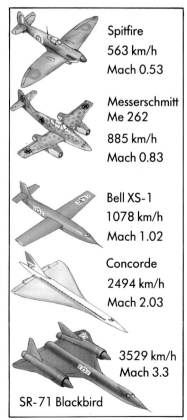

Spitfire
563 km/h
Mach 0.53

Messerschmitt Me 262
885 km/h
Mach 0.83

Bell XS-1
1078 km/h
Mach 1.02

Concorde
2494 km/h
Mach 2.03

3529 km/h
Mach 3.3

SR-71 Blackbird

Otto von Guericke (1602–1686)
Von Guericke was a German physicist and engineer who in 1650 invented the first air pump (used in the Magdeburg spheres) and later, the first electric generator. With the pump he was able to study objects in a vacuum. For instance, he showed that sound needs air to travel in and that air is essential for burning.

▶ *In his experiment von Guericke joined together two hollow hemispheres, pumped out the air and then tried to get two teams of horses to drag them apart. They did not succeed.*

Macintosh, Charles *See* Rubber

Magdeburg spheres

The Magdeburg spheres were two hollow halves of a copper sphere 35.5 cm in diameter, made by Otto von Guericke who lived in Magdeburg. He used them to demonstrate how the atmosphere exerts PRESSURE inwards on any surface. Normally we do not notice this, because there is also air, or some other FLUID, on the inside of the surface pushing outwards to balance the inward force. However von Guericke, who had invented the first air pump, was able to remove the air from inside the sphere formed from the two halves. They only felt the inward air pressure force (roughly equal to the weight of a 3 tonne lorry) so they could not be pulled apart.

SEE FOR YOURSELF
Put a piece of aluminium foil at the bottom of a plastic cup to prevent the plastic from getting scorched. Soak a piece of blotting paper in water, light a match and drop it on to the foil in the cup. Quickly, put the blotting paper on top of the cup and place the other cup upside down exactly on top of it. Pick up the top cup when the match has gone out. The bottom cup should be attached to it because as the match burnt it used up some of the air, giving a partial vacuum.

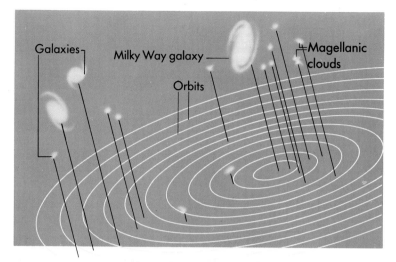

◀ The Magellanic clouds are part of the larger group to which our Milky Way galaxy belongs. All these galaxies are moving through space. The Magellanic clouds can be seen in the night sky in the Southern Hemisphere. Through a powerful telescope they can be seen to contain millions of stars (below).

Magellanic clouds

These two 'satellites' of our MILKY WAY galaxy are the nearest galaxies in space. They were discovered around 1520 by the Portuguese adventurer Magellan when he sailed the southern seas. With the naked eye they look like hazy glowing patches. They can only be seen from near the equator, or in the Southern HEMISPHERE.

The Large Magellanic Cloud is about 180,000 LIGHT-YEARS away and contains about 10,000 million STARS (about a tenth as many as our galaxy). The Small Magellanic Cloud is 230,000 light-years away and contains fewer stars. Both clouds contain bright NEBULAE where stars are being formed.

Magnesium

▼ Magnesium burns with an intense white light, used in fireworks and flares.

Magnesium is a chemically reactive, light, silvery-white metallic ELEMENT. It exists in such crystalline minerals as dolomite and magnesite and is found in sea water. Magnesium is an ingredient of CHLOROPHYLL and helps in various biological processes in plants and animals. Magnesium burns in air with an intensely bright, white flame. Because of this it is used in FIREWORKS and flares and was once used in photographic lighting. Magnesium exposed to air forms a greyish oxide coating, which protects the metal from further CORROSION. Because of its lightness, it is used in ALLOYS with such metals as aluminium and zinc, for building aircraft and cars. Magnesium is refined by various means, including ELECTROLYSIS. Magnesium oxide is heat-resistant and is used to line furnaces.

▶ *A maglev train is used as a shuttle to carry passengers and their luggage between the terminals of large airports.*

▼ *Magnetic tape is used in audio and video tape recorders and in some types of computers. It consists of a plastic tape with a coating containing magnetic particles. Before recording, the particles have a random arrangement. After recording, they have a regular pattern, corresponding to the recorded signal. The recording head is an electromagnet energized by the signal to be recorded. It arranges the particles into patterns, which can be made random again by the erase head.*

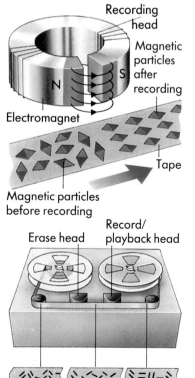

Recording head

Magnetic particles after recording

Electromagnet

Tape

Magnetic particles before recording

Erase head

Record/ playback head

Magnetic levitation (Maglev)

Magnetic levitation is a way of lifting objects by using the FORCES that keep MAGNETS apart. Train designers use magnetic levitation to make trains that float above their tracks. The train carries powerful LINEAR MOTORS which push against magnets laid in the special track. The magnets in the track first attract the train, pulling it forwards, and then, when it has passed, the direction of their magnetic fields is reversed, repelling the train and pushing it forwards even faster. Since the train floats above the track, there is no contact between the two. There are no moving parts such as wheels to wear out and there is no FRICTION between the train and the track. Using magnetic levitation, a Japanese experimental train, the MLU-001, travelled at 400.7 km/h in 1987. It is used for studies of future passenger trains.

Magnetic tape

Magnetic tape is a strip of flexible PLASTIC with a magnetic coating used to record SOUND and pictures. To make a recording, the TAPE is wound past an ELECTRO-MAGNET (the *recording head*). The magnetic field it produces varies with the sounds or pictures that created the field. The changing field moves magnetic particles in the tape as it passes the head. To play the recording, the tape is wound past the same head again. This time, the pattern of magnetic particles in the tape makes electric currents flow in the head that match the currents that created them. The recording can be erased by destroying the pattern of magnetic particles on the tape.

MAGNETISM

Magnetism is the force that acts between certain objects at a distance or when they are touching. There are two types of magnets—*permanent magnets* and *electromagnets*. An ordinary bar magnet will pick up and support nails or other bits of iron and steel. Its magnetism is strongest at its ends—its poles. If a piece of iron or steel is stroked in one direction with the bar magnet, the piece becomes a magnet too. If we place two bar magnets on a table, the north poles if placed close together will push each other apart. So will the south poles. But north and south poles will attract each other.

An electromagnet can be made by winding a coil of wire around a bar of iron and passing an electric current through the wire. The strength of the magnet increases with the number of turns in the coil and with the strength of the electric current. Electromagnets can be made more powerful than ordinary magnets and are used around the home in TV sets, tape recorders and telephones, as well as in huge industrial motors.

Two wires carrying electric currents in the same direction will attract each other magnetically.

▶ Magnets come in various shapes and sizes, including flat and round bars, rings, discs and horseshoe magnets. Magnets can transfer their magnetism temporarily to other magnetic materials. When a magnet is held near a magnetic material, its magnetic force causes the particles in the material to line up, giving the material magnetic properties.

▼ Magnets exert invisible forces through their poles. The lines of force of the magnetic fields can be 'seen' if iron filings are sprinkled on to some paper on top of the magnets. The iron filings follow the lines of force showing that these are concentrated at the magnets' poles and that like poles repel each other and unlike poles attract.

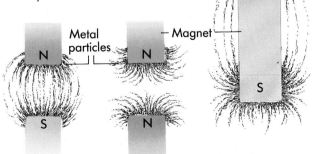

Metal particles — Magnet

William Gilbert (1540–1603)
Gilbert was physician to Elizabeth I and James I. He was the first to use the terms magnetic pole and electrical force, and suggested that the Earth's magnetism could be explained if the Earth was likened to a huge bar magnet. He thought (wrongly) that the planets held their orbits around the Sun by magnetic forces.

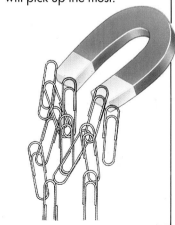

See also COMPASS; ELECTRICITY; ELECTROMAGNET; FORCE; GENERATOR; GEOMAGNETISM; MATERIALS; METALS; PHYSICS; POLES.

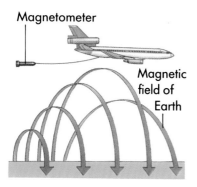

▲ A magnetometer can be towed behind an aircraft to detect the changes in the Earth's magnetic field that indicate the presence of minerals.

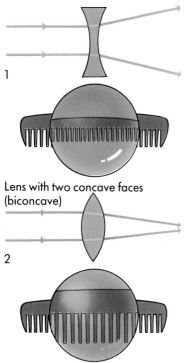

Lens with two concave faces (biconcave)

Lens with two convex faces (biconvex)

▲ The image produced by a concave lens **1** is smaller than life size. A convex lens **2** produces a magnified image. The difference is due to the different ways the two lenses bend light rays that pass through them.

▶ A magnified image of the threads in nylon stockings.

Magnetometer

A magnetometer is a device which is used to measure the strength of a magnetic field. The simplest type of magnetometer is a tiny coil of wire, which when moved through a magnetic field produces an electric voltage. Measuring this voltage indicates the strength of the field. More sensitive magnetometers, such as optically pumped magnetometers, can measure weaker magnetic fields. They can be towed behind aircraft to measure slight changes in the Earth's magnetic field. These changes help to locate deposits of iron, oil and other RESOURCES. Superconducting magnetometers are used to measure tiny magnetic fields in the human body .

Magnification

Magnification is the amount by which an image or picture of an object appears larger or smaller (a magnification of less than one). For example, a map or plan is usually smaller than in real life and it is necessary to know the magnification or scale in order to use it.

Optical instruments such as the MICROSCOPE and the TELESCOPE produce magnified images. The magnification that it is possible to obtain is limited by the quality of the LENSES or MIRRORS used, and by the DIFFRACTION of the LIGHT that passes into the instrument, which affects the instrument's resolving power (its ability to separate closely-spaced details). Magnification can be increased by using waves of shorter WAVELENGTH than light. Since ELECTRONS behave like waves which have much smaller wavelengths than light, an electron microscope has much higher magnification than an optical microscope.

Malleability

Malleability is a characteristic of many METALS by which they can be pressed or hammered into thin sheets. The best-known malleable metals are copper, gold and lead. Gold, for example, can be beaten into very thin sheets of gold foil or gold leaf just two microns (a micron is one millionth of a millimetre) thick so that light shines through it.

Malleable metals are also ductile, that is, they can be stretched out into thin wires without breaking. Malleability and DUCTILITY are due to the molecular structure of the metal concerned. The framework or lattice of the solid structure can be changed a lot before the energies holding the atoms together are overcome and broken. When this happens, the metal breaks. Some metals are only malleable when heated.

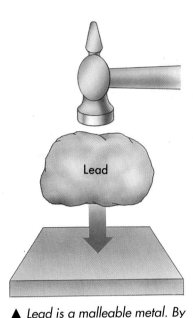

▲ Lead is a malleable metal. By hitting a lump of lead repeatedly with a hammer it can be beaten out into a thin sheet. Gold is the most malleable metal of all.

Malnutrition See Nutrition

Manganese

Manganese is a brittle, silvery-grey metallic ELEMENT found naturally in many MINERALS, including pyrolusite, manganite, braunite and hausmannite, and in iron ore. The manganese is usually found as a COMPOUND with oxygen and so has to be extracted.

Small amounts of manganese are essential to plants and animals. At high temperatures, manganese reacts with carbon dioxide and carbon monoxide and even burns in nitrogen (which is very unreactive). About 95

Some areas of the ocean floor are covered with potato-sized manganese nodules. They occur at depths of more than 2000 m and are most common in the Pacific Ocean. In addition to manganese, the nodules contain other metals such as copper and nickel.

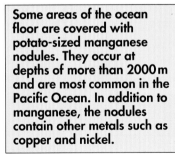

◄ Manganese is added to iron to make alloy steels that are extremely hard. Manganese steel is used for making the rails in railway crossings and the rollers in machines for crushing rock.

percent of all manganese used in industry is used by the IRON AND STEEL industry. It is used in STAINLESS STEEL and in alloys of aluminium and copper. Manganese dioxide is used in dry cell batteries and in dyes. Manganese sulphate is used in paints and varnishes and in fertilizers. Potassium permanganate is an efficient disinfectant.

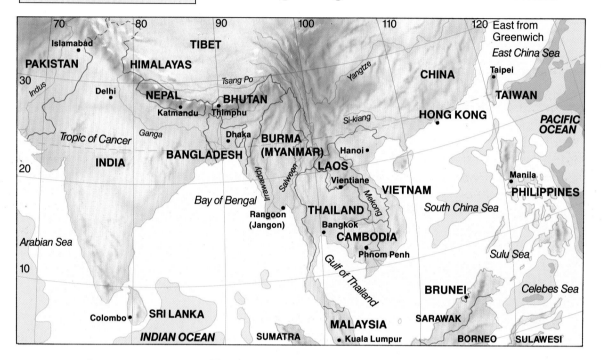

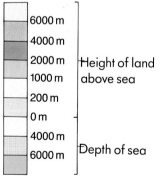

▲ There are many different kinds of maps. The map above is a relief map, showing the height of the land, the depth of the sea, and major rivers. It is also a political map as it shows countries, their boundaries, and their capitals.

Map

A map is a means of depicting on a two-dimensional flat surface the size, shape and features of a three-dimensional tract of land. The shape of the land surface is often represented by contour lines (joining points of equal height above sea level). Roads, railway lines, paths, rivers and so on are depicted by lines of different colours and thicknesses. Cities, towns and villages are shown, as are forests, airfields or reservoirs. A *relief map* is a scaled-down, three-dimensional model of the land's surface features, or relief. It gives an idea what the land's hills, valleys and vegetation may look like.

To make a map, it is necessary to carry out an accurate survey of an area of land. Today, map-making is aided by aerial photography and surveys from SATELLITES. Maps may be drawn to different scales; that is, the length of line on the map which is used to depict a distance on the ground of, say, 1km, may vary and is often represented by 2cm on the map (scale 1:50,000).

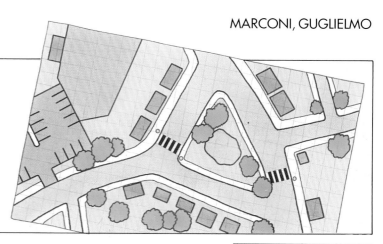

Map projections

Map projections are the way in which the curved surface of the earth is represented on a two-dimensional map. It is not possible to project a three-dimensional object such as the Earth onto a flat surface, just as the skin of an orange cannot be laid out flat.

The best that can be done produces a *projection* that is inaccurate in one direction, area or distance. It is thought that the Greek geographer, Ptolemy was first to suggest a projection. His work was forgotten about until the 16th century, when the Flemish map maker and geographer, Gerhardus Mercator (1521–94), found Ptolemy's ideas and developed a map projection with a rectangular grid which is still called a Mercator projection. The Mercator projection is still used for navigation but the shapes of large areas, such as Alaska, Greenland and Antarctica, are distorted and the scale on the map varies with latitude. For example, Iceland looks seven times as big as it would if it were on the equator. Different projections are used depending on what shape, direction, distance or area must be preserved accurately.

Marconi, Guglielmo

Guglielmo Marconi (1874–1937) was the Italian scientist who invented a system for sending messages (in Morse code) long distances without wires. He began experimenting with transmitting RADIO waves in 1894, having read about the work of Heinrich Hertz in producing electric waves. By inventing the ANTENNA and improving his receivers, he succeeded in sending bursts of radio energy over about 2.5 km. He increased the range of his transmissions to 15 km and set up a land station in Italy to communicate with warships (20 km) at sea. In 1899

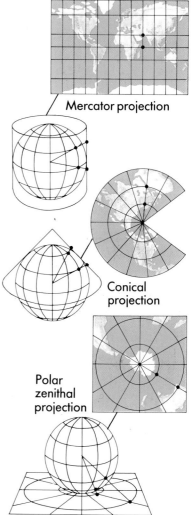

Mercator projection

Conical projection

Polar zenithal projection

▲ *In a Mercator projection, Earth's features are projected onto a cylinder, which is them unrolled to form the map. A conical projection uses a cone, and a zenithal projection uses a flat sheet.*

▲ *Marconi developed long-distance radio broadcasting.*

▼ *Margarine is made mainly from vegetable oil. First the oil is mixed with water and, after being purified, neutralized and having natural colours removed, it is reacted with hydrogen. This reaction, carried out using a catalyst, converts the liquid oil into a solid fat. The fat is then deodorized, vitamins and colouring are added, and the resulting mixture is blended with milk products. The finished margarine is squeezed into packets. Low-fat margarines contain a higher proportion of water.*

British warships succeeded in communicating over 120 km. In 1901, Marconi sent radio messages from Poldhu in Cornwall, to St. John's, Newfoundland — the beginning of worldwide radio COMMUNICATIONS. Marconi was awarded the Nobel Prize for Physics in 1909.

Margarine

Margarine is an artificial food used instead of butter. It is mainly a mixture of vegetable oils and milk products. It may also contain salt and FOOD ADDITIVES including flavouring, preservatives and colouring. Some margarine contains less FAT than butter and, particularly, less CHOLESTEROL, which can cause heart disease.

Margarine was invented in the late 1860s by a Frenchman, Hippolyte Mège-Mouriès. Its flavour was improved in 1903 by replacing some of the milk and a hard animal fat called suet in its recipe by vegetable oils obtained from plants. In 1944, during World War II, Britain began growing sunflowers as a source of oil for margarine and other foods. The flower contains hundreds of large seeds which are crushed to produce the oil. Sunflower oil is still used in some margarines.

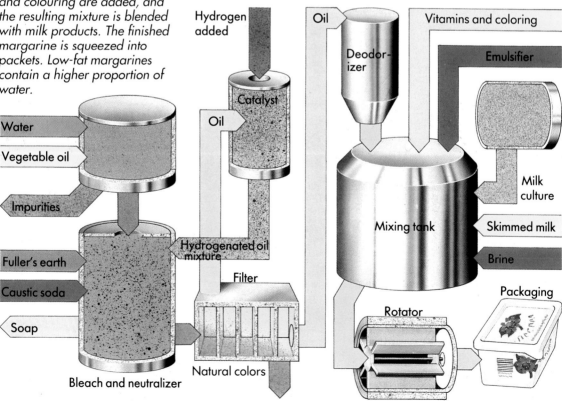

Mars Facts
Diameter 6794 km
Distance from Sun
249,000,000 km maximum
207,000,000 km minimum
Year length 687 d
Day length 24 h 37 min
Mass 0.11 of Earth
Density 0.71 of Earth
Surface temperature
−30°C maximum
−100°C minimum

Mars

Mars is the PLANET nearest the EARTH. It is much smaller and far colder, and its atmosphere is very thin. Its mountains and valleys are higher and deeper than anything on Earth, evidence of violent surface upheavals when it was younger. Its highest peak, Olympus Mons, rises 23 km above the desert, while its largest valley, Valles Marineris, is 4000 km long (the width of the USA), 75 km wide, and in places 7 km deep!

The photographs taken by the two Viking landers in 1976 showed a stony, dusty landscape. Dust is blown up and carried for thousands of kilometres by storms. The ice deposits around the poles melt and form again as the seasons change. The thin atmosphere is mostly carbon dioxide, and when the Sun sets the temperature drops.

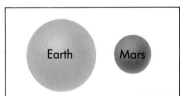

▲ Mars is half the size of the Earth but has a mass of only a tenth of Earth's.

▼ The surface of Mars is covered with craters, volcanoes and gorges. Two of the largest are the volcano Olympus Mons and the gorge called Valles Marineris.

Giovanni Schiaparelli (1835–1910)
Schiaparelli was an Italian astronomer who believed he could see narrow lines on Mars. He called them 'channels', meaning rivers or river beds. But his Italian word *canali* was mistranslated as 'canals', meaning artificial waterways. American space probes have proved that there are no canals on Mars.

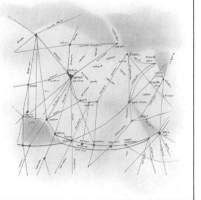

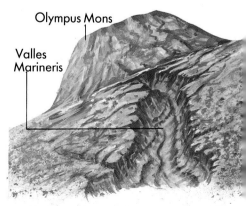

Olympus Mons

Valles Marineris

▶ *Much of the surface of Mars looks like a red, stony desert. This photograph was taken by a Viking Space probe in 1976.*

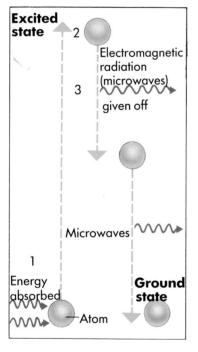

Excited state

2

Electromagnetic radiation (microwaves)

3

given off

Microwaves

1

Energy absorbed

Atom

Ground state

▲ *In a maser, 1 atoms are excited by firing bursts of energy at them. 2 Excited atoms lose this energy and 3 return to their original or ground state in two stages. Microwaves are released as the atom changes from one energy level to the lower one.*

There may be water permanently frozen below the surface. Some features which look like old water-channels have been photographed, and could mean that millions of years ago Mars was warmer, with liquid water. If this is true, there might have been life as well.

Mars has two tiny satellites: Phobos and Deimos. The larger, Phobos, measures only 27 km from end to end, and they are both irregular in shape. Phobos is only 6000 km above the surface of Mars, and its 'month' (the time it takes to go around Mars once) is 7 hours 39 minutes! It is gradually spiralling inwards, and in about 40 million years it will crash into Mars.

Maser

A maser produces an intense beam of ENERGY. 'Maser' stands for Microwave Amplification by Stimulated Emission of Radiation. (Microwaves have WAVE-LENGTHS of only a few centimetres.) In 1954, the American Charles H. Townes described how a maser might work: the ATOMS of a gas might be energized or 'excited' by firing pulses of energy at them. They release their excess energy as an amplified burst of microwaves. The first maser was made at the Bell Laboratories in the United States in 1956. Because a maser produces waves at a precise frequency, it can be used as a clock.

Masers are used as AMPLIFIERS in satellite communications and radio astronomy. As soon as the maser was successfully developed, scientists searched for its optical equivalent. The result was the LASER.

Mass

The mass of an object is the amount of material it contains. It determines two important things about a body: first its INERTIA, in other words how large a FORCE is needed to produce an ACCELERATION. (How much force do you need to push a stationary car?) If the mass of a body is doubled, so is its inertia. A bus has more inertia than a car. Second, the mass determines how strongly the force of GRAVITY attracts the body to other objects. The force of gravity towards the Earth is the WEIGHT of an object, so the mass also determines the weight. But mass and weight are different. Weight gets smaller the farther away from Earth you are. Mass remains the same. (Astronauts in space are weightless but their mass is always the same.)

Einstein's theories of RELATIVITY tell us that mass is a form of ENERGY; an object travelling at 257,500 km/s has twice the mass as it had when it was standing still.

▲ Mass never changes, but weight depends on the force of gravity. The Earth is not perfectly round; it is wider at the equator than the poles. So while at the North Pole 1 kg mass weighs 9.83 newtons (N), at the equator it weighs 9.78N.

Mass number

The mass number is the total number of PROTONS and NEUTRONS in an ATOM. All atoms of a particular ELEMENT have the same number of protons at their centre, but they may have different numbers of neutrons. These atoms with different numbers of neutrons are called ISOTOPES. For example, in one isotope of uranium called U-235, there are 92 protons and 143 neutrons (92 + 143 = 235). In U-238, there are 92 protons and 146 neutrons. Their mass numbers are 235 and 238 respectively. *See also* ATOMIC WEIGHT.

▲ The mass number of an element is the total of the protons and neutrons in its atomic nucleus. Carbon atoms have 6 protons and 6 neutrons, and a mass number of 12.

Mass spectroscopy

Mass spectroscopy is used in chemical ANALYSIS to detect what ELEMENTS are present in a compound or mixture and to find out which ISOTOPES of an element are

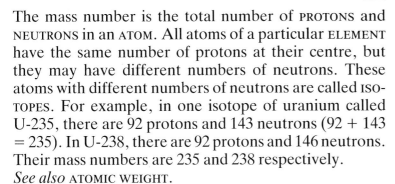

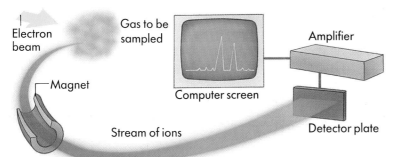

◀ In a mass spectrometer, the atoms in a gas mixture are converted to ions by electron bombardment. The stream of ions passes through a magnetic field, which separates them by curving the paths of some ions more than others, depending on their masses.

The importance of materials in the lives of people can be seen by the names given to major periods in history. More than 2 million years ago the Stone Age began, followed by the Bronze Age and then the Iron Age. By the mid-1700s, steel was the new material. Today, new materials appear every day. We could say that we are living in the Materials Age!

present in a sample. A machine called a mass spectrometer bombards a sample with ELECTRONS, thus producing IONS in the sample. The ions can be separated from each other by their MASS or electric charge. The ions are passed through an electric field, which separates them by the strength of their charges, and then through a magnetic field, which deflects the heavier ions more than the light ones. The ions are now spread out to give a pattern called a mass spectrum. Ions from each element produce unique patterns, so the elements in the sample can be identified.

Materials

Materials are substances used to make things. They may be natural or synthetic (man-made) or a mixture of the two. The first materials used by people were natural. Clothes were made from woven FIBRES from plants, and furs or skins from animals. Tools were carved from wood or animal bones, or by chipping away at a rock to make sharp-edged cutting tools. Homes were made from animal skins, leaves or mud fixed to a wooden frame. All these materials were obtained quite easily and were given little or no processing. But often a suitable natural material is not available or not strong enough.

People learned how to produce new materials. From ORES found in the Earth's surface, METALS were extracted. New building materials were made from clay blocks fired in a furnace or KILN. Sand was used to make GLASS. During the 20th century, scientists began to make

▲ Plastic is an artificial material with many uses. A special kind of light (polarized light) produces rainbow colours where there are strains in this moulded plastic bottle.

▶ A modern racing yacht uses many different materials, from wood and metal to fibreglass and plastic for the hull and polymers for the sails and ropes. For example, a strong material called kevlar is used in sails and ropes (and also in bullet-proof jackets!).

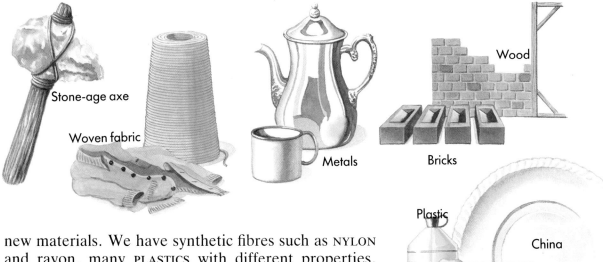

Stone-age axe

Woven fabric

Metals

Bricks

Wood

Plastic

China

Rubber

Glass

new materials. We have synthetic fibres such as NYLON and rayon, many PLASTICS with different properties, some transparent like glass but less brittle, others good electrical INSULATORS or resistant to heat. Making anything, from a shirt or COMPUTER to a motor vehicle or house, requires an understanding of how materials behave in order to choose the best materials.

Mathematics $\sqrt{}$

Mathematics is the name of a group of sciences concerned with number, quantity, shape and place and their various relationships. Learning to count and work with amounts, shapes and angles is one of humankind's major achievements. *See* pages 432 and 433.

▲ *Through the ages, people have had more and more materials to make things from. At first, there were only stones and wood. Today there is a whole range of synthetic materials, such as plastic and nylon, in addition to all the natural ones.*

Matter

Matter is all the material in the UNIVERSE. There are several STATES OF MATTER; the matter around us on Earth is made up of ATOMS in the form of SOLIDS, LIQUIDS and GASES. At very high temperatures, the electrons of an atom can become separated from its nucleus and a fourth state of matter called plasma is formed. The Sun and other stars are made of plasma.

Astronomers can only detect matter in the Universe directly if it gives off LIGHT or some other form of ELECTROMAGNETIC RADIATION which can be detected. Matter which cannot be seen in this way is often referred to as 'dark matter'. Dark matter can still be detected because its GRAVITY produces forces on other objects. At present it seems that there must be a very large amount of dark matter in the Universe.

> The three normal states of matter are solids, liquids and gases. Most substances can exist in all three states, depending on the temperature. At low temperatures they are a solid. If the solid is heated, it eventually melts to form a liquid. At even higher temperatures, the liquid boils to form a gas or vapour. At extremely high temperatures, such as that in the Sun, there is a fourth state of matter called a plasma.

MATHEMATICS

Ancient Egyptians used arithmetic and geometry to measure out plots of land and to build the pyramids with great accuracy more than 5000 years ago. Arithmetic deals with numbers and calculating. Addition, subtraction, multiplication and division are its four main operations. Geometry is concerned with lines, angles, figures and solids. Greeks such as Euclid worked out most of the general principles of geometry, called theorems, about 2500 years ago. Algebra is a kind of mathematical shorthand that uses symbols such as *x* and *y* to stand for unknown quantities. It was developed by the Arabs less than 1200 years ago in the 9th century. Arithmetic, geometry and algebra are the foundations of mathematics.

Mathematics is the language of science. Engineers, physicists and other scientists all use mathematics. Other experts, who are interested in numbers, quantities, shapes and space for their own sake, use pure mathematics. Number theory, the study of whole numbers and how they behave, is a typical branch of pure mathematics. In the modern world, mathematics is a key element in electronics and computing.

Milestones in Mathematics
3000 BC Ancient Egyptians use geometry for land surveys and for building.
300 BC The Greek mathematician Euclid uses logic to work out theorems in geometry.
800s Arab mathematicians invent algebra.
1100s Arabic numerals introduced into Europe.
1514 John Napier invents logarithms.
1680s Sir Isaac Newton and Gottfried von Leibnitz independently develop calculus.
1820s Charles Babbage begins building a mechanical computer.
1854 George Boole develops Boolean algebra for solving logic problems.
1960s Schools begin teaching new maths, such as set theory.
1970s–1980s Thematical models are used on computers for studying engineering problems, to predict changes in weather patterns and so on.

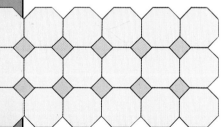

◀ *Only regular shapes with fewer than seven sides will fit together alone to make a pattern with no gaps. This is called tessellation. Squares, equilateral triangles (six of which make a hexagon) and hexagons (six-sided regular polygons, the shape of bees' cells) will all tessellate. Octagons (eight sides) will tessellate with squares.*

▶ *Before the electronic calculator was developed, people used a slide rule to make quick calculations. The numbers on a slide rule are arranged logarithmically. Napier invented logarithms in the 16th century and for hundreds of years the use of tables of logarithms enabled accurate multiplication and division of large numbers.*

Spider Paths
A spider wants to walk both ways along each edge of a cube without going along the same path twice. You can show the cube on a piece of paper as in the diagram on the right. The clever spider starts along the base of the cube (1), and so on.

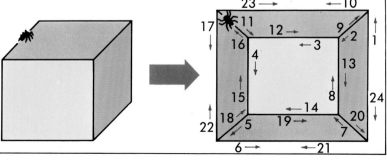

432

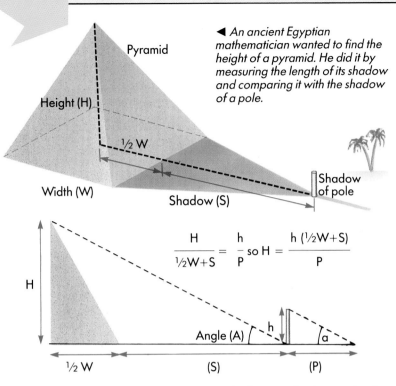

Pyramid

Height (H)

½ W

Width (W)

Shadow (S)

Shadow of pole

◀ *An ancient Egyptian mathematician wanted to find the height of a pyramid. He did it by measuring the length of its shadow and comparing it with the shadow of a pole.*

$$\frac{H}{\tfrac{1}{2}W+S} = \frac{h}{P} \quad \text{so } H = \frac{h\,(\tfrac{1}{2}W+S)}{P}$$

H

½ W

Angle (A)

h

a

(S)

(P)

▲ *Here is how the mathematician did the calculation. First he added half the width of the pyramid (½W) to the length of the pyramid's shadow on the ground (S) to give the total length of the shadow (½W + S). He then measured the length of the pole's shadow (P). He could measure the height of the pole directly (h). He then reasoned that the height of the pyramid (H) divided by the total length of the*

shadow must be the same as the height of the pole divided by the length of its shadow. Knowing three of these lengths, he was able to calculate the fourth. You can try this for yourself using a tall object such as a tree or a building and a pole that you have measured to find length.

Powerful Mathematics

To square a number, you multiply it by itself. For example, 10^2 is $10 \times 10 = 100$. We have raised 10 to the power 2. To cube a number, you multiply it by itself twice. For example, 10^3 is $10 \times 10 \times 10 = 1000$. We have raised 10 to the power 3. Similarly, $10^1 = 10$ and $10^0 = 1$ (any number to the power 1 equals the number; any number to the power 0 equals 1). You can also use negative powers. For example, $10^{-1} = 1 \div 10 = 0.1$ and $10^{-2} = 1 \div 100 = 0.01$.

Mathematicians call a power an index (plural indices). Indices are useful for expressing very large or very small numbers. For example, the speed of light is about 300,000,000 metres per second, written as 3×10^8 m/s. Avogadro's number is about 6×10^{23} or 6 followed by 23 zeros. The minute particle called an electron that makes up part of an atom is very small. It weighs about 9×10^{-28}g or 9 divided by 10 followed by 27 zeros.

SEE FOR YOURSELF

Statistics are facts and figures about a particular subject, such as the type and number of vehicles that use a certain road. They can often best be presented in the form of a graph, such as a bar chart. Make a list of the kinds of different vehicles that use the road where you live, and count how may of each kind pass in a particular time. Then draw a bar chart like the one shown here.

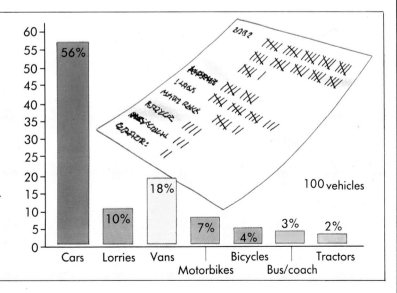

100 vehicles

Cars	56%
Lorries	10%
Vans	18%
Motorbikes	7%
Bus/coach	4%
Bicycles	3%
Tractors	2%

See also ALGEBRA; ARITHMETIC; BABBAGE, CHARLES; CALCULATOR; COMPUTERS; ELECTRONICS; GEOMETRY; MEASUREMENT; NUMBERS; STATISTICS

People have been using the mechanics of pulleys for hundreds of years. It is said that Hieron II, King of Syracuse, challenged Archimedes to demonstrate the power of simple machines that the great scientist had been boasting about. Archimedes arranged a system of pulleys which allowed him single-handedly, to pull a fully-laden ship out of the water and on to dry land.

Maxwell, James Clerk *See* Electromagnet

McClintock, Barbara *See* Genetics

McMillan, Edwin *See* Uranium

Measurement

People need to know how big something is, how much it weighs, how much space it takes up, and so on. A farmer needs to know how much land he has for planting a certain amount of grain. These questions can be answered by measurement. *See* pages 436 and 437.

Mechanics

Mechanics is the part of PHYSICS which deals with the way objects move in response to the FORCES between them. The laws which govern the mechanics of everyday objects around us were discovered by Isaac NEWTON more than three hundred years ago; he showed how forces cause the MOMENTUM of an object to change. He also showed how the force of GRAVITY, which is responsible for the WEIGHT of objects on the Earth, also causes the planets to orbit the Sun. The laws of mechanics are important for the design of machines.

Although Newton's mechanics correctly predicts how planets and objects of everyday sizes behave, it cannot correctly explain the behaviour of very small objects such as ATOMS. A new type of mechanics, QUANTUM MECHANICS, is needed to explain this.

▼ Mechanics involves the application of Newton's three laws of motion. These state that: 1 an object at rest remains at rest unless acted on by a force. Also an object moving in a straight line continues to do so unless acted on by a force. 2 When a moving object is acted on by a force, its rate of change of momentum is proportional to the force and in the direction of that force. 3 When two objects interact, the force exerted by the first (the action) results in a corresponding force by the second (the reaction). Action and reaction are equal and opposite.

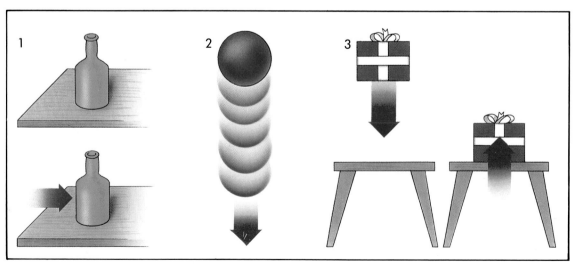

MEDICINE

Medicine is the science and art of healing. There are dozens of specialized branches of medicine such as cardiology (treatment of disorders of the heart), dermatology (treatment of diseases of the skin), orthopedics (treatment of disorders of the skeleton and muscles) and pediatrics (treatment of children's diseases).

Medicine has been practised since the earliest recorded time. Clay tablets describing medical treatment were found in Babylon (3000 BC). In Europe and the Middle East, medicine was influenced by the ancient Greeks and later preserved by Arab and Jewish doctors, who continued to improve on the older knowledge. In fact, apart from some surgery, up to the end of the 18th century there was very little that a doctor could do for a patient, and many of the 'cures' were worse than the disease. Now medicine is a true science, and every drug or technique that the doctor uses must be carefully tested and proved to work. The modern doctor makes a diagnosis on the basis of signs, which can be seen; symptoms, which the patient describes; and often, pathology reports on material from the patient that has been sent to a specialized laboratory to be tested. Most medicine is aimed at treating illness or damage with drugs or surgery. Many doctors now undertake preventive medicine, which is aimed at keeping the body healthy.

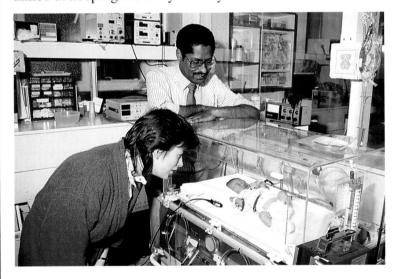

▲ A baby that is born early or which has a very low birth weight may be cared for in an incubator. Inside the incubator, the temperature and the oxygen content of the air can be carefully controlled. The parents may not be allowed to touch their baby very often to reduce the risk of infection.

Milestones in Medicine
2000 BC Medicine practised in China and India.
1651 William Harvey describes the circulation of the blood.
1700s John Hunter perfects surgical techniques.
1846 William Morton uses ether as an anesthetic.
1895 Wilhelm Roentgen discovers X-rays.
1920s Frederick Banting and Charles Best use insulin to treat diabetes.
1960 Albert Sabin develops oral polio vaccine.
1967 Christiaan Barnard carries out the first human heart transplant.
1985 Lasers are used during surgery to clean out clogged arteries.

Robert Koch (1843–1910)
Koch was a German doctor who founded bacteriology, the study of bacteria. He identified the bacteria that cause such diseases as anthrax, cholera and tuberculosis. He also studied malaria and concluded that it is caused by mosquito bites, at the same time as the British doctor Ronald Ross. Koch received the 1905 Nobel Prize in Medicine.

Alternative Medicine
Some doctors use holistic (whole-body) methods. These can be special diets or medical techniques such as acupuncture and osteopathy.

See also DISEASE; DRUGS; HIPPOCRATES; PAIN; PATHOLOGY; PSYCHOLOGY AND PSYCHIATRY; TRANSPLANTS; VETERINARY MEDICINE; X-RAYS.

MEASUREMENT

Measurement is the process of comparing something unknown with something known and generally accepted. The thing that is known becomes a standard from which we can derive units that are used for direct measurements.

In early history, parts of the body and other daily examples were taken as units. The yard, foot and inch were based on parts of the body, the furlong (220 yards) was the length of furrow an ox could plough without a rest, and an acre (4840 square yards) the area that the ox could plough in a day. Since these quantities were not standard they were not reliable measurements. In time, fixed standards were agreed on for the various measures. In the 1790s during the French Revolution, scientists in Paris developed the metric system, based on the centimetre, gram and second (cgs system). It was adopted for scientific purposes in Britain in 1852, but this system was inconvenient when defining electrical and magnetic quantities, so in 1901 the Italian engineer Giovanni Giorgi suggested a system based on the metre, kilogram and second (mks system). This became the basis of the Système International d'Unités (SI units), which was adopted by an international conference in 1960.

Scientists and instrument-makers ensure that instruments give accurate readings by marking, or calibrating, the scale in appropriate units. A mercury thermometer can be calibrated for 100°C in the following way. First, it is placed in water that is just boiling. A mark is made on the glass parallel with the top of the mercury: 100°C, the boiling point of water. Later the thermometer is placed in water in which ice is forming and a mark is made in line with the top of the mercury: 0°C, the freezing point of water.

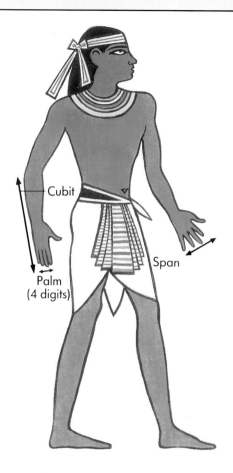

▲ *Many measurements of dimensions (height, width, depth and breadth) were originally based on parts of the body. The Egyptians used the palm (equal to 4 digits), the span (a handspan) and the cubit (length of forearm).*

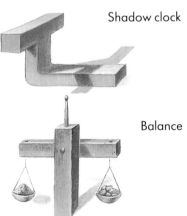

Shadow clock

Balance

▲ *A micrometer is used to make very accurate measurements, such as the diameter of high-precision metal tubes.*

▲ *Early methods of measuring included the shadow clock, which told the time by the position of a shadow along a bar, and a beam balance which weighed things against known weights.*

Area and Volume
The length of a straight line is measured in metres or sometimes in smaller (millimetres) or larger (kilometres) parts of metres. Ordinary metres cannot be used to measure areas or volumes. A square with sides of one metre has an area of one metre times one metre or one square metre ($1\ m^2$). A cube with sides of one metre has a volume of one metre times one metre times one metre or one cubic metre ($1\ m^3$).

Anders Ångström (1814–1874)

Ångström was a Swedish physicist who studied light and the spectrum of the Sun. In 1868 he discovered hydrogen in the Sun's spectrum. He gave his name to a very small unit of length (the ångström), used for measuring the wavelengths of light and the distances between atoms. There are ten thousand million ångströms in a metre.

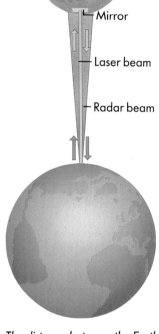

Mirror

Laser beam

Radar beam

▲ *The distance between the Earth and the Moon can be measured accurately by timing how long it takes a laser beam to reach the Moon and be reflected back again (astronauts left a mirror there). A radar beam spreads out as it travels, and so is not as accurate.*

SEE FOR YOURSELF

You can measure length using a chain of paperclips, and mass using glass marbles. You could call your units 'clips' and 'marbles'. A cup may be 3 clips tall and weigh 12 marbles. You can measure time by painting stripes round a candle and counting them as the candle burns down.

SEE FOR YOURSELF

A clinometer is used to measure angles in surveying. You can make your own by taping a drinking straw and a protractor to a piece of cardboard. Hang a small weight from a thread at the protractor's centre. Look along the straw and read off the angle on the scale.

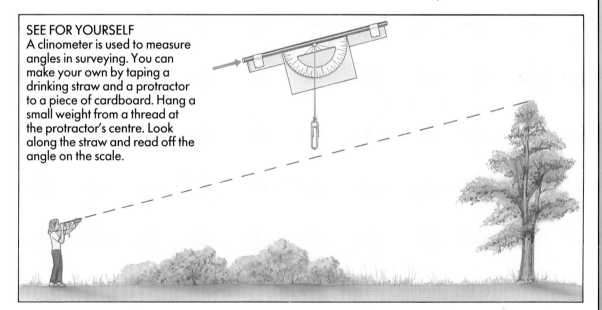

See also INSTRUMENTS, SCIENTIFIC; METRIC SYSTEM; MICROMETER; SCALES AND BALANCES; SI UNITS; THERMOMETER; WEIGHTS AND MEASURES.

Meiosis *See* Cell division

Meitner, Lise *See* Nuclear energy

Melting point

Melting point is the TEMPERATURE at which a SOLID turns into a LIQUID. For pure elements such as copper or simple compounds such as water, the melting point is the same as the FREEZING POINT. When a solid is heated so that it melts, the molecules vibrate rapidly and partly overcome the forces that hold them in their positions. They can move around but cannot break away completely from each other. Pure elements or compounds melt at a precise and definite temperature. Mixtures melt over a wider range of temperatures. For example, zinc melts at 419.58°C, while copper melts at 1083.4°C. Together they form brass with a melting point that ranges from 900° to 1000°C.

> Some solids do not melt to a liquid when heated; they change directly from a solid to a gas. This process is called *sublimation* and happens to such substances as camphor, iodine and arsenic.

> ▶ The melting point of a solid is the same as the freezing point of its liquid; ice melts at 0°C and water freezes at the same temperature. The chart shows the melting points of various substances. Helium turns to a gas at temperatures above −269°C, and solid mercury melts at −38.9°C.

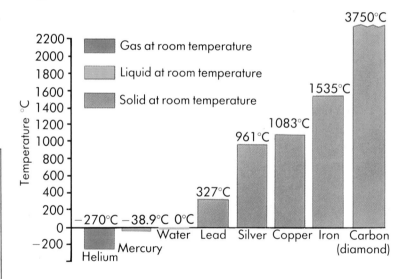

Memory

Memory is the ability to store information so that it can be recalled for use later. Computers are said to have a memory as well as animals.

Although some small areas in the BRAIN are known to play an important part in memory the function is spread around the brain, making it difficult to study how it works. There are several types of memory. One is called sensory storage, and lasts for a very short time. It allows us to take in what the eye sees, and then almost

> Nobody really knows how memories are stored in the brain or how we recall them when we want to. (Or why we cannot remember some things when we try hard to do so.) Memories probably involve chemical changes in groups of nerve cells in the brain. These changes affect the ways the cells connect together and how messages pass between them. When a group of nerve cells are used again and again, they develop more connections between each other, allowing them to pass messages better. When cells lose their connections because they are not used, memory fails and we forget things.

SEE FOR YOURSELF

A party game that tests memory is called Kim's Game. The organizer puts various objects on a tray and shows it to the players. After one minute the tray is removed, and the players have to make a list of the objects. A trick is to make mental connections between objects. For example, make yourself remember that there are two things beginning with 'c' (comb and cup) and two beginning with 's' (scissors and spoon). If two of the things have the same colour, remember that fact.

Many people think they can improve their memory by practising remembering things. This is not so; but we can help our ability to remember by using mental aids such as rhymes, mental pictures, clues and other devices. How many of us would remember the days in each month without the rhyme 'Thirty days has September...'?

immediately fades away. If we think about the picture we have been looking at, or the sound we have heard, it becomes part of our *short term memory*. If you meet someone new only once their face or name will quickly disappear from the short term memory. But if you see them frequently, or repeat their name a number of times, it is transferred to the *long term memory*, and may be remembered for years. The more you refer to a stored memory, the more firmly established it becomes. Moving experiences into the long term memory is part of the LEARNING process which starts after birth.

Mendel, Gregor *See* Heredity

Mendeleyev, Dmitri *See* Periodic table

Meniscus

The meniscus of a LIQUID is the upper surface of the liquid contained in a partly filled narrow tube. The meniscus of a liquid is curved and is caused by SURFACE TENSION. The meniscus may be upward-curving (convex) or downward-curving (concave). When measuring liquids against scales, the reading should be taken from

▼ *Mercury is a liquid metal with a very high surface tension. This can be seen by comparing the surface of mercury in a test-tube with the surface of water. With water, the meniscus, the shape of the surface, curves upwards at the edges where the liquid is in contact with the tube. With mercury, the meniscus curves downwards.*

Water   **Mercury**

▶ *The meniscus on a liquid forms a sort of skin and is caused by surface tension. Many insects and other animals take advantage of this 'skin' which enables them to walk on water, just as this raft spider is walking on the surface of a pool.*

the middle of the meniscus. Meniscus (from the Greek for 'crescent') is also the name for a LENS that is convex on one side and concave on the other.
See also CAPILLARY ACTION.

Mercury compounds are poisonous and can cause mental illness. At one time felt for making hats was manufactured from rabbit fur. Mercury salts were used to remove the hairs from rabbit skins, and people who did this job gradually became poisoned by mercury. This is the origin of the expression 'as mad as a hatter'.

Mercury

Mercury is the only metallic ELEMENT that is a LIQUID at ordinary room temperatures. People have known of mercury since ancient times, its silvery colour and the fact that it flows easily, earning it the name quicksilver.

Mercury is obtained by heating a bright red ore called cinnabar, a COMPOUND of mercury and SULPHUR. Mercury expands at a constant and even rate when heated and contracts evenly when cooled. It stays liquid from −38.87°C to +356.58°C and so has been widely used in THERMOMETERS and BAROMETERS. It conducts electricity and is used in batteries, switches and ELECTROLYSIS cells. A current passing through mercury VAPOUR 'excites' the atoms and makes them give out ultraviolet and visible light. The ultraviolet light is filtered out in street lights, but some is retained for sunbeds where it helps tanning.

▶ *Droplets of mercury look like tiny polished metal domes because the liquid metal acts as a curved mirror and reflects light.*

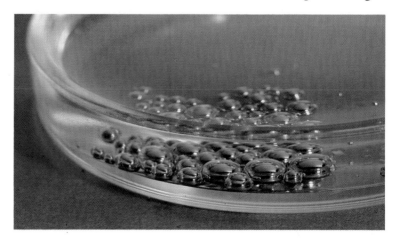

Mercury Facts
Diameter 4878 km
Distance from Sun
70,000,000 km maximum
46,000,000 km minimum
Year length 88 d
Day length 59 Earth days
Mass 0.055 of Earth
Density 0.98 of Earth
Surface temperature
450°C maximum
−170°C minimum

◀ *Mercury is the planet nearest the Sun, which it orbits every 88 days. Daytime temperatures reach 450°C.*

Mercury (planet)

The innermost PLANET of the SOLAR SYSTEM, Mercury has been visited by one spacecraft, Mariner 10 in 1974. Its camera shows an atmosphereless cratered world rather like the MOON. This was expected, though Mercury is hard to study from the Earth; only Pluto is smaller, and Mercury's weak GRAVITY could not hold on to any gases to form an atmosphere.

The SUN beats down furiously on Mercury as it slowly rotates, taking over two months to pass from sunrise to sunset. During this time the surface heats up to 450°C, but during the long night the temperature falls to about −170°C, as cold as icy Saturn!

There are two main differences between the surfaces of Mercury and the Moon. Mercury has no dark, dusty plains, and the surface is wrinkled, as though the underlayers have shrunk, leaving the outer skin slightly too large. A huge body must have crashed into Mercury several thousand million years ago, causing a circular area 1300 km across, known as the Caloris Basin.

Most of the planets have orbits that are almost circular, but Mercury's is an obvious ellipse. Its distance from the Sun changes from 70 million km when farthest away to only 46 million when nearest, so that from Mercury the Sun sometimes appears one and a half times the diameter (and feels twice as hot) as at others.

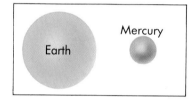

▲ *Mercury is not much larger than the Moon and is the smallest planet after Pluto, the outermost planet.*

▼ *The surface of Mercury is pitted with thousands of craters left after meteors crashed into the planet.*

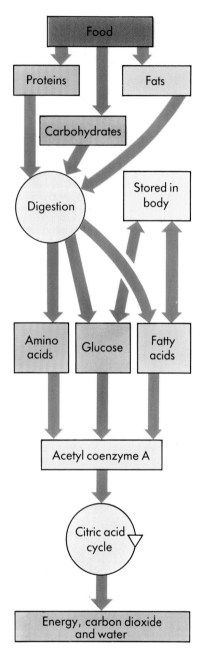

▲ All the processes of metabolism are controlled by enzymes. They include the breakdown of food during digestion, the storing of food products, and the use of these products to supply energy and build up new tissues.

Metabolism

Metabolism is a term used to describe all the chemical processes taking place in an organism. All these processes use ENERGY. Plants use the Sun's energy to build simple molecules such as water and carbon dioxide into sugars which they store for energy. Animals take in complicated molecules in their food and release the energy in them by breaking them down. This energy can then be used with simpler substances, like those produced by digestion, to build up into more complicated molecules needed by the body for growth or repair. All metabolic processes need ENZYMES, chemicals that speed up reactions. Without enzymes, metabolic processes would be very slow or would not take place at all.

The speed at which the food is burned or metabolized to produce energy is called the metabolic rate. This varies from individual to individual. In humans, it is greater in children than in adults. Because our energy requirements are all different, so the amount of food we need is different too.

See also PHOTOSYNTHESIS; RESPIRATION.

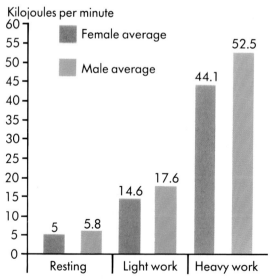

◀ The rate at which the body uses energy varies, depending on how hard we work. It is also different for males and females. When doing heavy work, we use up energy nine times as fast as when we are at rest.

Metal detector

A metal detector is used to find metal objects buried in the ground. It works by transmitting radio waves down into the ground. Any metal object will interfere with these waves by absorbing some of them and reflecting fewer back to the detector. The reflected waves are picked up by the detector's receiving circuit which

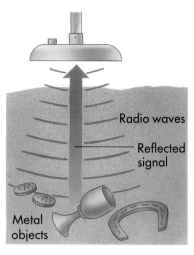
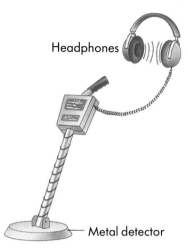

Headphones

Radio waves

Reflected signal

Metal objects

Metal detector

◄ *A metal detector locates buried metal objects by sending out radio waves and picking up any signals reflected off the objects. An electronic circuit linked to headphones converts the reflected signals into high-pitched sounds.*

amplifies them into a strong signal that tells the user of the object's presence. When the object interferes with the radio waves it changes the frequency of the signal and therefore the note heard.

Metal fatigue

Metal fatigue is the progressive weakening of METAL. It is usually caused by the repeated pushing, pulling or other buffeting of a component during the normal use of a machine. The stresses that the component undergoes in ordinary use often change the arrangement of the molecules in the metal. Too much stress can pull the molecules apart and cause the metal to break. Minor defects in the metal's surface provide a place where stress can build up and start to crack the metal. All metals that bear a load or are shaken up a lot will suffer from metal fatigue. Engineers must allow for it when designing and building aircraft, bridges and machinery.

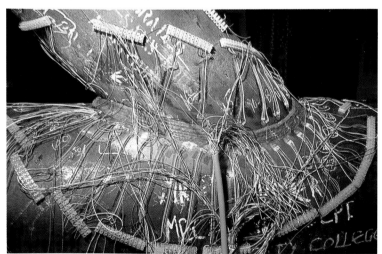

◄ *Stress in metal can lead to dangerous metal fatigue. For this reason, engineers test a metal structure. Here part of a pipeline has been surrounded with electronic gauges to measure stresses and strains.*

▲ *Physical metallurgists may study the behaviour of metals under great stress. This piece of metal has been greatly magnified to show a fracture. By studying the breaks in metals, metallurgists are able to understand more about their structure and how to reduce the chances of them breaking.*

▼ *Metals have many uses. Precious metals such as gold and silver are used for making jewellery. Base metals like iron and steel are important in construction and for making cars and ships. Tin and zinc give protective coatings. Useful alloys include brass, bronze and aluminium alloys.*

Metallurgy

Metallurgy is the branch of CHEMISTRY that studies METALS. There are two types of metallurgy: *extractive metallurgy* and *physical metallurgy*. Extractive metallurgy deals with the various ways in which metals are separated from their ORES. Physical metallurgy is the study of the structure and properties of metals.

Metallurgists use microscopes to check for surface flaws in metals. From their analyses, they can find out how best to protect metals from the effects of RUST, other CORROSION and METAL FATIGUE. The improvement and strengthening of metals for use in manufacturing includes such processes as making ALLOYS, heat treatment (such as the tempering or annealing of steel), ANODIZING, ELECTROPLATING, GALVANIZING and carburizing (adding carbon to a metal). The formation of the metal into its final shape by hammering, casting, rolling or extrusion (stretching) is also a part of physical metallurgy. Recent developments in the science include the study of materials called composites, in which metals are combined with fibreglass or plastic.

Metals

A metal is an ELEMENT, such as sodium, gold or zinc, with certain properties. Most metals are shiny, all except mercury are solid at room temperature, and most have the qualities of MALLEABILITY and DUCTILITY.

About 80 metals are known. Most can be found in the EARTH's crust. Few occur in a pure state. Most are

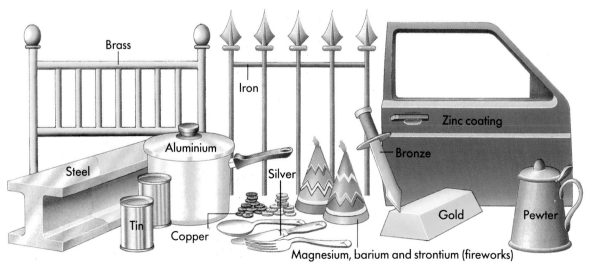

Brass

Iron

Zinc coating

Aluminium

Bronze

Steel

Silver

Tin

Gold

Pewter

Copper

Magnesium, barium and strontium (fireworks)

combined with other elements in rock-like deposits called MINERALS and ORES that are removed from the Earth by mining and other methods. They can be separated from their ores, but such REFINING often uses large amounts of ENERGY. The most common method of separating metals from their ores is smelting in a BLAST FURNACE.

Pure metals are rarely used, but in solid mixtures called ALLOYS (such as bronze or steel) they provide hard, strong, long-lasting materials for all sorts of building, construction and manufactured goods. These alloys are often referred to as metals. Small amounts of certain metals are essential to plants and animals. Iron for animals' blood cells and calcium for teeth and bones are particularly important.

Metals are good conductors of heat and electricity because the electrons of a metal are able to move around more easily than those of a non-metal. Metal atoms join together to make up larger units called CRYSTALS that have a regular structure.

Metamorphic rocks

Metamorphic ROCKS have been changed during their formation in terms of texture, chemical composition or in the MINERALS from which they are made. The change may be brought about by a rock being subjected to heat, or pressure, or both. Metamorphic rocks may originally have been IGNEOUS ROCKS, SEDIMENTARY ROCKS, or even a different kind of metamorphic rock. The process which forms metamorphic rocks is known as *metamorphism*. For example, a large body of igneous rock may be

Slate

Marble

Gneiss

Cordierite hornfels

▲ Metamorphic rocks include slate, used for roofing, and marble, which can be carved and polished. In gneiss there are bands of light and dark minerals, and cordierite hornfels is a fine-grained silicate rock.

◄ Sometimes boulders of metamorphic rocks such as gneiss are embedded in an otherwise sandy area.

445

▶ *Metamorphic rocks are formed by the action of heat and pressure on sedimentary rocks within the Earth's crust. The sedimentary rock limestone, for example, can be changed into the metamorphic rock marble; both are forms of the mineral calcium carbonate. Soft clay minerals are changed into slate and shale. Large crustal movements that form mountains cause large scale regional metamorphism, whereas an intrusion of molten igneous rock may bring about thermal metamorphism.*

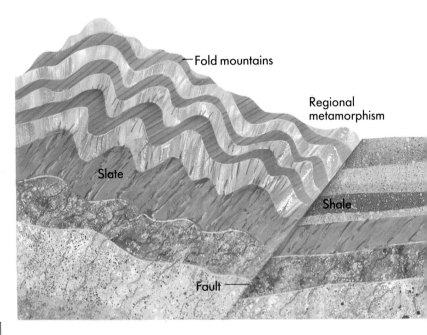

Fold mountains

Regional metamorphism

Slate

Shale

Fault

The metamorphosis of frogs is controlled by the thyroid gland, a small gland in the neck. If this gland is removed from the tadpole or if there is no iodine for the gland to function properly, then the frog just keeps growing in its tadpole state and never metamorphoses.

intruded into the surrounding rocks or the rocks may be subjected to heat and pressure as a result of major mountain-building events in the processes of PLATE TEC-TONICS. Marble is metamorphosed limestone while a hard, crystalline rock, called quartzite, is sandstone that has been metamorphosed.

Metamorphosis

A butterfly spends the early part of its life as a wingless caterpillar called a LARVA. The amazing change from the crawling, leaf-eating larva to the flying, nectar-sucking adult is called metamorphosis. Many other animals, including crabs and frogs, undergo metamorphosis, although the change is not always as striking as that shown by the butterfly. Larvae usually live in different habitats from the adults and commonly feed on different foods. This is a very useful arrangement because it means that more individuals of one SPECIES can live in one area than

▼ *A butterfly is an insect that undergoes complete metamorphosis. An egg hatches into a caterpillar, which changes its skin several times as it grows before becoming a pupa. After a few weeks the pupa splits open and the adult butterfly emerges. At first its wings are limp and shrivelled, but they soon enlarge and harden in the sunlight.*

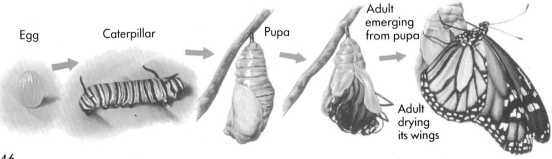

Egg   Caterpillar   Pupa   Adult emerging from pupa   Adult drying its wings

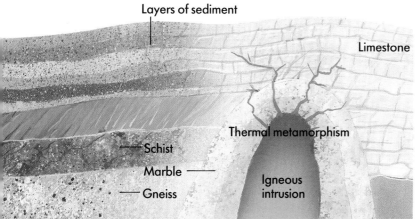

Layers of sediment

Limestone

Thermal metamorphism

Schist

Marble

Gneiss

Igneous intrusion

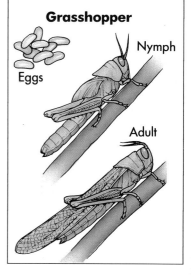

Incomplete Metamorphosis

Some insects, such as earwigs and grasshoppers, pass through only three stages of metamorphosis. The egg hatches into a nymph, which resembles a small adult but has no wings. The nymph changes its skin (moults) several times as it grows. At the last moult, an adult winged insect emerges.

Grasshopper

Eggs

Nymph

Adult

would be possible if they all fed on the same foods.

Metamorphosis is controlled by HORMONES which circulate in the body. A caterpillar, for example, contains supplies of juvenile hormone which ensure that it stays a caterpillar for a while. But when it is time to change to a butterfly the supply of juvenile hormone stops, and when it next changes its skin the caterpillar becomes a *chrysalis* or pupa. Injecting juvenile hormone into caterpillars causes them to stay as caterpillars.
See also METAMORPHIC ROCKS.

Meteor

A meteor is a particle sometimes as small as a sand grain hurtling at up to 40 km/s into the atmosphere. Most meteors burn up above an altitude of 100 km. If you gaze at the stars for half an hour on a clear night, you will see an occasional streak of light, which is a meteor's glowing trail.

Meteor particles (known as meteoroids) are fragments of MATTER orbiting the SUN like minute planets. They originate from the beginning of the SOLAR SYSTEM, or are thrown out by COMETS. Meteoroids from comets usually travel in swarms with many kilometres between each tiny particle. When the Earth passes through a swarm, a 'meteor shower' is seen. Regular meteor showers are seen on the same date each year, when the Earth returns to the swarm. Some of the best occur around January 4, August 12 and December 13.

▲ A meteor is a small object that enters the Earth's atmosphere and burns up.

▶ *A meteorite is a traveller from outer space, a lump of stone or metal that has survived being burned up as it rushes through the Earth's atmosphere to crash to the ground.*

Meteorite

Meteorites are bodies from space that are large enough to reach the ground without burning up in the atmosphere as METEORS do. The largest known meteorite weighs about 60 tonnes and landed in Namibia, southern Africa. About 25,000 years ago, an object about 100 m wide fell in Arizona, producing a crater 1200 m across.

A falling meteorite will leave a brilliant trail in the sky known as a 'fireball', but very few meteorites have been found by tracking fireballs. Since they can look like ordinary dark stones, most meteorites have been discovered by special searches in areas where they stand out, such as the snowfields of Antarctica.

Some meteorites are mostly metal (iron and nickel), while others are made of stone. These may be fragments from ASTEROIDS that later broke up in collisions.

Meteorology

Meteorology is the study of WEATHER over a relatively short period, by looking at temperature, rainfall, air pressure, hours of sunshine, and so on. Climatology, the study of CLIMATE as a whole, is concerned with long-term weather patterns. *See* pages 450 and 451.

Meters, electricity and gas

Electricity and gas meters are instruments used to measure how much ELECTRICITY or NATURAL GAS an appliance has used. An electricity meter consists of a rotating metal disc with ELECTROMAGNETS above and below it. The size of the magnetic fields produced by the electromagnets depends on the amount of electricity used. The fields interact with the metal disc and make it rotate. The number of turns it makes are counted automatically and appear as a number on the meter.

A gas meter works by pumping the gas alternately through two chambers. As each fills and empties in turn, levers attached to the valves of the containers drive a counter which shows the amount of gas used as a number of units.

Methane

Methane, or marsh gas, is a colourless, odourless, non-toxic, highly flammable GAS. It is a HYDROCARBON which is made up one atom of CARBON to every four atoms of HYDROGEN. It is the simplest of the alkanes, a series of hydrocarbons that includes PROPANE.

Methane is a natural product of rotting vegetation in marshes and bogs and some mammals produce it during DIGESTION. It is used as a FUEL and is the main ingredient of the NATURAL GAS used in homes for heating and cooking. It is also the main gas in firedamp that causes explosions in mines.

Methane is the starting point for the commercial production of several chemicals, including hydrogen, carbon monoxide and hydrogen cyanide. Methane makes up a large part of the atmospheres of the giant planets Jupiter, Saturn, Uranus and Neptune.

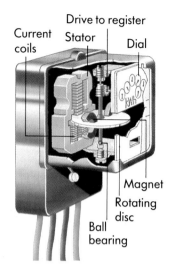

▲ An electricity meter measures electricity used in kilowatt-hours, also called units.

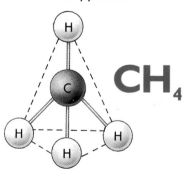

▼ A methane molecule is shaped like a triangular-based pyramid. It has a carbon atom in the middle, bonded to four hydrogen atoms located at the corners of the pyramid.

◄ Methane is produced when dead plants rot. This process can be used to make the gas for use as a fuel. Here a submarine-shaped tank is filled with leaves and plant waste, and methane is tapped off through a pipe.

449

METEOROLOGY

The patterns of the weather have long been important to people, especially farmers, whose crops, animals and therefore livelihoods depend upon them. In the days of sailing ships, being able to predict the weather could be the difference between a speedy voyage to a distant land or shipwreck in a storm. So, farmers and sailors were among the first to forecast the weather by observing its patterns.

Even though weather satellites now provide much of the information on which forecasts are based, weather stations still supply important data, especially at a local level. A typical weather station might include a barometer to measure air pressure, a maximum/minimum thermometer to record the highest and lowest temperatures, an anemometer and wind vane to measure wind speed and direction, a rain gauge to measure the amount of rainfall, and a hygrometer to measure the humidity of the atmosphere.

Satellites and computers are vital to modern weather forecasters. The computers use information from the satellites to predict the global weather patterns over various periods of time. There are two main kinds of satellite but both make their observations using ordinary visible light during the day and infrared radiation at night. One kind of satellite which is in a geostationary orbit, orbits directly above the Earth's equator at the same speed as the Earth rotates. This means that it is effectively stationary and can take pictures of the same place at intervals of, for example, thirty minutes. The other kind of weather satellite rotates the Earth from pole to pole so that, because the Earth is rotating, it takes observations of successive strips of the planet between the North and South Poles.

Cloud cover measured in eighths (oktas)

Symbol	Value
○	0
◑	1 or less
◕	2
◔	3
◐	4
◑	5
◕	6
◖	7
●	8
⊗	Sky obscured
⊗	Missing or doubtful data

Weather

=	Mist	▽	Rain shower
≡	Fog	*	Rain and snow
'	Drizzle	▽	Snow shower
•	Rain	▽	Hail shower
*	Snow	K	Thunderstorm

Wind speed (knots)

◎	Calm		8 – 12
	1 – 2		13 – 17
	3 – 7		48 – 52

▲ *Meteorologists use various symbols to indicate cloud cover, weather and wind speed. For winds over 17 knots, each extra 'feather' adds 5 knots.*

Weather Lore

There are many sayings about the weather and some have a basis in truth. For example, 'Red sky at night, shepherd's delight. Red sky in the morning, shepherd's warning'. In the Northern Hemisphere, when the sky in the west (after sunset) is red, the air is clear and dry. Most of the weather comes from the west and so the next day is likely to be fine and dry. A red sky in the morning occurs when the Sun lights up ice particles in the air, and rain clouds are likely to follow.

◀ *Scientists at the South Pole send up instruments suspended from a balloon to study weather conditions in the upper atmosphere.*

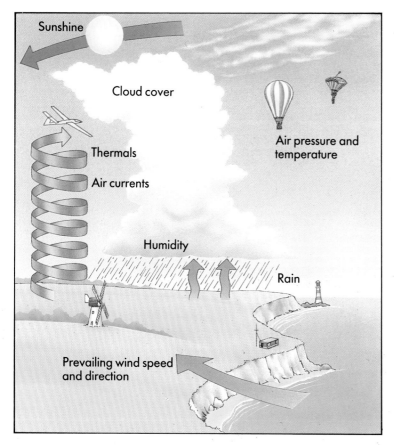

Sunshine

Cloud cover

Thermals

Air currents

Air pressure and temperature

Humidity

Rain

Prevailing wind speed and direction

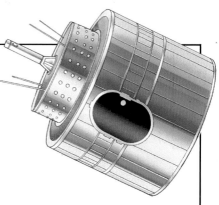

▲ *Artificial satellites such as Meteostat orbit the Earth and send back photographs of cloud formations. Using these pictures meteorologists can watch the development of a weather system, such as a hurricane, track its direction and warn people of its approach.*

◄ *The chief factors that affect the weather, and are therefore measured in order to prepare weather forecasts, are air pressure, air temperature and the speed and direction of the wind.*

SEE FOR YOURSELF

To estimate wind speed and direction, you can make a wind sock. Cut a long strip of paper and string it up on a tall stick or pole. An anemometer can be made from four plastic cups and the top of an old plastic bottle, using thin canes and a knitting needle. A rain gauge can also be made from a plastic bottle.

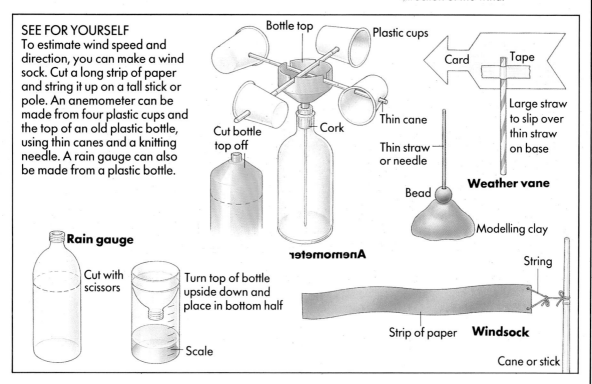

Bottle top

Plastic cups

Card

Tape

Cut bottle top off

Cork

Thin cane

Thin straw or needle

Large straw to slip over thin straw on base

Bead

Weather vane

Modelling clay

Anemometer

Rain gauge

Cut with scissors

Turn top of bottle upside down and place in bottom half

Scale

String

Strip of paper   **Windsock**

Cane or stick

See also ANEMOMETER; BAROMETER; FRONT, WEATHER; HUMIDITY; HURRICANE; PRECIPITATION; SATELLITE, ARTIFICIAL; WEATHER; WIND.

The metric system, so-called because it began with the metre, is a decimal system of units. Multiplying or dividing numbers by 10 is easy because it only involves changing the position of the decimal point. Arithmetic has not always been this easy. Until recently measurement of length was based on 12 inches in a foot and 3 feet in a yard and then 1760 yards in a mile – three totally different number systems.

Metric Prefixes	Symbol	Multiplication		Power of 10	
tera-	(T)	×	1,000,000,000,000	=	10^{12}
giga-	(G)	×	1,000,000,000	=	10^{9}
mega-	(M)	×	1,000,000	=	10^{6}
kilo-	(k)	×	1000	=	10^{3}
hecto-	(h)	×	100	=	10^{2}
deca-	(da)	×	10	=	10^{1}
deci-	(d)	×	0.1	=	10^{-1}
centi-	(c)	×	0.01	=	10^{-2}
milli-	(m)	×	0.001	=	10^{-3}
micro-	(µ)	×	0.000001	=	10^{-6}
nano-	(n)	×	0.000000001	=	10^{-9}
pico-	(p)	×	0.000000000001	=	10^{-12}

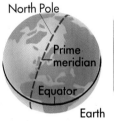

North Pole / Prime meridian / Equator / Earth / Platinum-iridium

▲ In the original metric system, the metre was defined as a ten-millionth of the distance between the North Pole and the equator, and a kilogram as the mass of a standard platinum-iridium cylinder.

▼ Mica is a mineral that consists of flaky layers that can easily be split apart to give very thin slices of rock.

Metric system

The metric system is a system of MEASUREMENT in which each successive multiple of a unit is ten times as large as the one preceding it. For example, 10 mm = 1 cm.

The system uses seven basic units of measurement whose values are fixed by reference to international standards. These units are the metre (length or distance), the kilogram (mass), the second (time), the kelvin (temperature), the ampere (electric current), the mole (amount of a substance) and the candela (intensity of light). Metric units have a prefix in front of them to indicate how they relate to the basic unit, whether they are multiples or fractions of the basic unit. French scientists devised this system in the 1790s. Since then it has been improved and the Système International d'Unités (SI UNITS) has been adopted in most countries.

Mica

Micas are a group of MINERALS which have a structure such that the atoms of SILICON and OXYGEN, of which micas are partly composed, are arranged in layers or sheets. Because the sheets of silicon and oxygen are held together only weakly, micas tend to have a flaky structure and split cleanly into sheets. The best-known micas are biotite, which is shiny black, and muscovite which is silvery and almost transparent. Biotite and muscovite are found in IGNEOUS ROCKS, such as granite, and in certain kinds of METAMORPHIC ROCKS especially the schists, where the micas give the rock a structure rather like the leaves of a book.

MICROBIOLOGY

Microbiology is the study of microscopic organisms, such as bacteria, viruses, moulds and yeasts. It is concerned with their classification, structure and function, and how they can be controlled and used. In 75BC, Lucretius believed that plague was caused by 'atoms', but it was not until the 18th century that Pasteur and Koch began to explore the part microorganisms play in causing disease. Pasteur noted the association of bacteria with fermentation and disease, and developed pasteurization to kill microorganisms. Koch demonstrated that particular bacteria could cause a particular disease, and developed ways of cultivating them in the laboratory.

Microbiology progressed quickly, helped by the invention of better microscopes and laboratory techniques. Since the 1940s, microbiology has progressed enormously, helped by the development of electron microscopes which reveal the detail of even the smallest microorganisms. Moulds, yeasts and bacteria have all been cultivated and changed by genetic engineering or selection of useful characteristics. They now produce antibiotics, substances mimicking those in the body, vaccines and antibodies.

▲ Microbiologists use chemical reagents and microscopes to study minute organisms such as moulds and bacteria.

Euglena

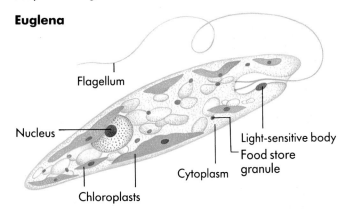

Flagellum

Nucleus

Chloroplasts

Cytoplasm

Light-sensitive body

Food store granule

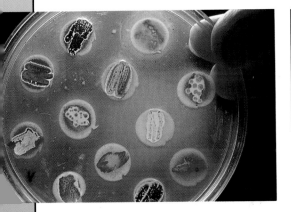

Antibiotics are products of microbiology. Penicillin was first made in quantity during the 1940s, when it became possible to cultivate the mould which produces it. Many antibiotics are now made synthetically.

▲ Euglena is a single-celled aquatic organism. It makes its own food by photosynthesis but eats other food when there is no light. It moves around by lashing its whip-like flagellum.

◀ Microorganisms can be grown or 'cultured' in a jelly-like substance in a glass dish. Scientists can then study the effects of drugs on the microorganisms.

See also BIOLOGY; DISEASE; DRUGS; FERMENTATION; GENETIC ENGINEERING; MICROORGANISM; MICROSCOPE; PASTEURIZATION; YEAST.

Microchips are able to perform at almost the speed of light – at more than a million operations per second. A microprocessor has the power of a large computer but is made up of only one integrated circuit held on a microchip. Early microprocessors could handle 50,000 to 100,000 operations per second – many fewer than they can nowadays.

Microchip

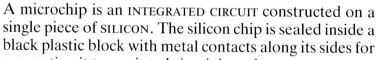

A microchip is an INTEGRATED CIRCUIT constructed on a single piece of SILICON. The silicon chip is sealed inside a black plastic block with metal contacts along its sides for connecting it to a printed circuit board.

The personal COMPUTER or microcomputer would be impossible without the miniaturization of electronic components that resulted in the microchip. A microchip can contain hundreds of thousands of individual electronic components. In the early days of computing in the 1940s and 1950s, this number of components would have filled several rooms. There are different types of microchips for different jobs. Memory chips store computer data. A MICROPROCESSOR controls a computer connected to other equipment by an interface chip.

▶ A microchip contains thousands of electronic components all mounted in a single block of plastic.

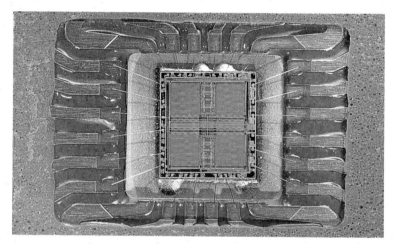

Micrometer

A micrometer is an instrument used to measure accurately the length, diameter or thickness of small items. It works on the principle that a screw moves forwards by a certain amount for every turn of the screw.

To measure the thickness of an object, the object is placed between in the jaws of the micrometer and the handle which contains the spindle and screw is tightened on it. The thickness of the object is then read off a scale on the micrometer's handle. Sometimes the scale can be difficult to read. To make micrometers easier to use accurately, some of the latest micrometers register the number of turns of the handle, and therefore the thickness of objects, electronically. The measurement appears as a LIQUID CRYSTAL DISPLAY.

▼ A micrometer measures small dimensions very accurately. Turning the thimble along a screw thread moves the spindle and uncovers a scale. The micrometer may also have a vernier scale which allows for even more accuracy.

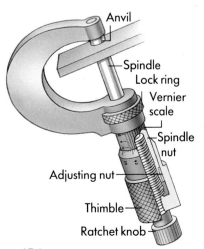

Anvil
Spindle
Lock ring
Vernier scale
Spindle nut
Adjusting nut
Thimble
Ratchet knob

Microorganism

A microorganism is a living ORGANISM which cannot be seen properly with the naked eye. A MICROSCOPE must be used to study it. There are several different groups of microorganisms: microscopic animals and plants, and bacteria, VIRUSES and some small fungi.

Bacteria have a very simple structure, usually with a cell wall to protect them from drying out. Huge numbers live in the SOIL, where they break down dead material and help it to decay. Many animals, including humans, have millions of bacteria living harmlessly in the gut, as well as on the skin. Only a few bacteria cause disease, such as Salmonella which causes one kind of food poisoning. Viruses are also microorganisms, but they cannot move, grow or reproduce on their own. They enter a living cell and combine themselves with the cell contents

The first person to see microorganisms was Anton van Leeuwenhoek, a Dutchman who ground lenses as a hobby. Leeuwenhoek spent hours peering through his simple lenses at flies, pieces of skin, and even scrapings from his teeth. Then, one day he examined a drop of dirty rainwater. In it he could see, as he wrote, 'Wretched beasties swimming and playing, a thousand times smaller than one can see with the eye alone.' This was the first sighting of bacteria made by humans.

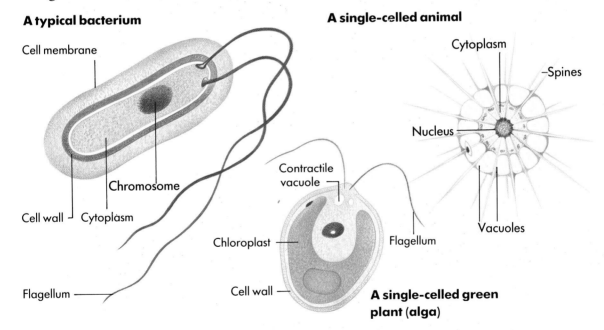

A typical bacterium

Cell membrane

Chromosome

Cell wall ⌐ Cytoplasm

Flagellum

A single-celled animal

Cytoplasm

–Spines

Nucleus

Vacuoles

Contractile vacuole

Chloroplast

Flagellum

Cell wall

A single-celled green plant (alga)

so they can take over the cell's activities. Viruses cause many diseases in animals and plants.

Protozoa are tiny animals, many of which live in water or in the soil, and a few of which cause serious diseases such as dysentery. A minute fungus called YEAST ferments sugar into alcohol and is used in wine and beer making, and also helps bread to rise. Other fungi are found in the soil and work like bacteria to break down dead material. Both bacteria and fungi are used to produce substances such as medicinal drugs.

▲ Microorganisms include bacteria and various single-celled animals and plants. All are too small to be seen by the naked eye and can be studied by using a microscope. Some microorganisms make their own food by photosynthesis in chloroplasts and others take in particles from around them. Some have flagella which they beat to move about.

455

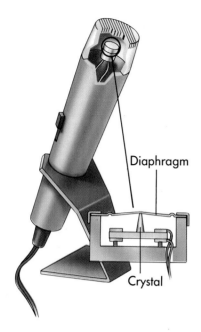

Diaphragm

Crystal

▲ *In a crystal microphone, sound waves vibrate a diaphragm whose movement squeezes a piezoelectric crystal. The pressure on the crystal makes it produce an electric current which varies in step with the vibrations.*

▶ *The heart of a microprocessor is a silicon chip integrated circuit, mounted on a base with two rows of pins or terminals. Microprocessors are used in automatic control systems for various machines, and may make up the chief components of a microcomputer.*

Microphone

A microphone changes SOUNDS into an electric current. Sound waves in the air strike a paper or plastic surface called a 'diaphragm' and make it vibrate in step with the sound waves. These vibrations are used to change the electric current flowing through an electric CIRCUIT. This can be done in different ways. A DYNAMIC MICROPHONE works like a LOUDSPEAKER in reverse. A coil of wire attached to the diaphragm vibrates in a magnetic field, causing an electric current to flow through the coil by electromagnetic INDUCTION. In a *carbon microphone*, the vibrating diaphragm varies the electrical resistance of a carbon contact. In a *condenser microphone*, it varies a property called CAPACITANCE in the circuit. A *crystal microphone* uses a PIEZOELECTRIC crystal to convert the vibrations directly to an electric current.

Microprocessor

A microprocessor is the control centre and ELECTRONIC calculator of a COMPUTER. It was introduced in the early 1970s by the US Intel Corporation; the first time a computer's central processing unit could fit on a single chip.

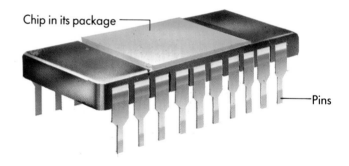

Chip in its package

Pins

The tiny size of the microprocessor enabled computer manufacturers to produce smaller, more powerful computers that were also less expensive than before. The microprocessor made the microcomputer possible.

Microscope

A microscope is an instrument used to produce a larger image of an object. Light shining through the object is bent by a LENS before it enters the observer's eye, making the object appear larger than it really is. By adding a second lens to magnify the image produced by the first,

Glass globes filled with water were probably used as magnifying glasses at least 3000 years ago. The Romans may have used clear crystals as magnifying glasses.

the image can be made even larger. Microscopes with more than one lens are called compound microscopes. The microscopes used by scientists to look at plant and animal cells are compound microscopes. In the 1930s, a new type of microscope called an ELECTRON MICROSCOPE was developed. It uses streams of ELECTRONS instead of LIGHT to give a higher magnification. The most powerful microscopes are scanning tunnelling microscopes. They also use electrons but in a different way and they can now magnify 100 million times.

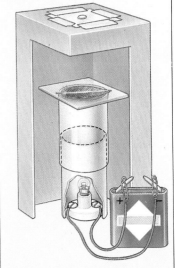

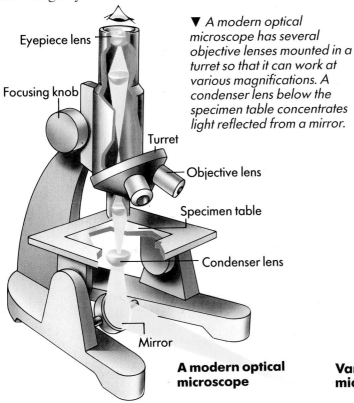

Eyepiece lens

Focusing knob

Turret

Objective lens

Specimen table

Condenser lens

Mirror

▼ *A modern optical microscope has several objective lenses mounted in a turret so that it can work at various magnifications. A condenser lens below the specimen table concentrates light reflected from a mirror.*

A modern optical microscope

Van Leeuwenhoek's microscope

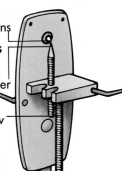

Lens

Specimen holder

Adjusting screw

▶ *This microscope is very different from modern ones. It had a single hand-ground lens. The specimen was placed on the pointed rod and viewed from the other side through the minute lens. The long screw moved the specimen into the line of sight.*

Anton van Leeuwenhoek (1632–1723)
Leeuwenhoek was a Dutch draper who also ground magnifying lenses and used them to study the things around him. He made his first microscope in the 1670s, and was later to become the first person to see bacteria, the cells that make up yeast and some blood cells. He lived to age 90 and during his life, he ground a total of 419 lenses.

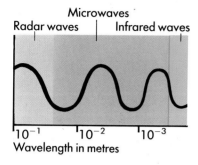

Microwaves
Radar waves | Infrared waves

10^{-1} 10^{-2} 10^{-3}
Wavelength in metres

▲ *Microwaves are a form of electromagnetic radiation with wavelengths between those of infrared and radar waves. They correspond to extremely high frequency radio waves.*

▶ *The heart of a microwave oven is a magnetron. This is a two-electrode valve that generates microwaves, which are usually reflected onto the food to be cooked. The waves agitate water molecules in the food. The molecules rub against each other and the friction produces heat, which cooks the food. Other parts of the oven consist of a timer and a switch to vary the output power of the magnetron.*

Microwaves

Microwaves are a form of ELECTROMAGNETIC RADIATION, typically with a WAVELENGTH of a few centimetres. They are used for communications, since their wavelength is a convenient size, easy to direct and control. Microwaves are usually produced from a metal cavity into which a whole number of wavelengths will fit exactly; this is very like the way in which SOUND is produced by an organ pipe. Very intense microwave beams can be produced using a MASER.

Microwaves can be used for cooking. In a microwave oven, the water molecules in the food absorb microwave ENERGY and so the food is heated through and cooks.

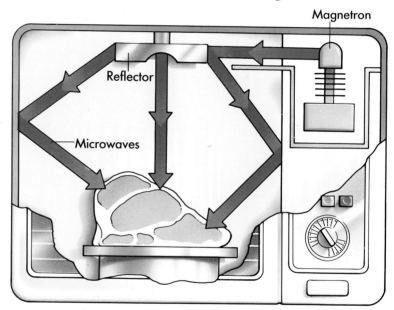

Magnetron

Reflector

Microwaves

Migration

Migration is the regular movement of animals to and from certain areas. It usually takes place at particular seasons. Swallows and many other birds, for example, spend the winter in tropical areas and then fly off to breed in cooler regions during the summer. By doing this they avoid the competition for food in the TROPICS and they have longer summer days in which to collect insects to feed their young. They return to the tropics for winter because there are not enough insects for them to eat in the cooler areas. Some birds fly thousands of kilometres between their summer and winter homes.

Many mammals also migrate. Humpback whales, for

In ancient times, people did not understand why some birds or other animals disappeared at certain times of the year. Some people thought that birds spent the winter in caves or in the mud of swamps and lakes. As recently as the 18th century, one writer tried to prove that birds flew to the Moon for the winter!

◀ *Monarch butterflies gather in their thousands before beginning their long flight down the west coast of North America.*

▼ *The map shows the distances travelled by some of the world's long-distance migratory animals. Most of them are birds, but also represented is an insect (the Monarch butterfly) and two mammals, the Caribou (reindeer) and the Blue whale.*

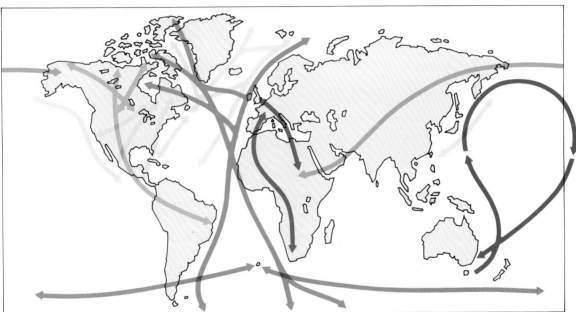

example, feed in the polar OCEANS but when winter comes they move to the tropical oceans to breed. Mountain mammals move to lower levels to escape the winter snows, and reindeer living in the far north move further south for the winter. European eels swim all the way to the Sargasso Sea in the western part of the Atlantic Ocean to lay their eggs. The baby eels then take three years to swim back to the European rivers.

Even insects migrate. Monarch butterflies fly all the way from Canada to Mexico to sleep through the winter. Immense swarms of locusts occasionally fly out from over-crowded areas to settle elsewhere, but as they do not return, we call these movements emigrations.

➡ Short-tailed shearwater

➡ Golden plover

➡ Arctic tern

➡ Blue whale

➡ Monarch butterfly

➡ Wandering albatross

➡ Cuckoo

➡ Wheatear

➡ Caribou

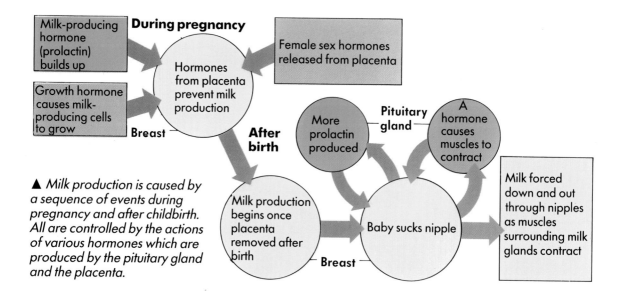

During pregnancy

Milk-producing hormone (prolactin) builds up

Growth hormone causes milk-producing cells to grow

Breast

Hormones from placenta prevent milk production

Female sex hormones released from placenta

After birth

More prolactin produced

Pituitary gland

A hormone causes muscles to contract

Milk production begins once placenta removed after birth

Breast

Baby sucks nipple

Milk forced down and out through nipples as muscles surrounding milk glands contract

▲ *Milk production is caused by a sequence of events during pregnancy and after childbirth. All are controlled by the actions of various hormones which are produced by the pituitary gland and the placenta.*

Each Western dairy cow produces about 4000 litres of milk a year. About two-thirds of our milk is drunk fresh; the rest is made into butter and cheese. Some people cannot digest a substance called lactose (milk sugar) which makes up about 5 percent of cow's milk.

Milk

Milk is the liquid food produced by a female mammal to feed her babies. It is formed in the mother's mammary GLANDS and starts to flow as soon as the babies are born. It contains water, FAT, PROTEIN, SUGAR, VITAMINS and MINERALS that the babies need for the first few days or months of their lives. The milk is different for each kind of mammal. Seal milk has a large amount of fat, so that baby seals can quickly build up a layer of fat or blubber under the skin to insulate them from the cold. Cows' milk is a valuable food for people, but not suitable for very young babies.

The milk we drink is heated for a short time to kill any dangerous bacteria. This is called PASTEURIZATION. It does not kill all the bacteria and after a few days the bacteria make the milk sour. People drink the milk of buffaloes, goats, sheep, reindeer, cows and other animals.

Milky Way Facts
Diameter 100,000 light-years
Thickness at centre 15,000 light-years
Speed of rotation once every 225 million years
Speed through space 2.2 million kilometres per hour
Age 15,000 million years
Estimated mass more than 100,000 million Suns

Milky Way galaxy

We exist in space in the company of about 100,000 million STARS and vast clouds of gas and dust called NEBULAE. This is our galaxy, and it measures about 100,000 light-years across. The SUN is about 30,000 light-years from the centre, and the Milky Way effect seen crossing a dark starlit sky is caused by the faint light from millions of stars in the galaxy's spiral arms.

Our galaxy probably began soon after the UNIVERSE, about 15,000 million years ago. To begin with it may

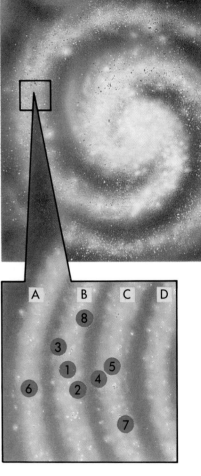

◀ The Milky Way galaxy consists of several spiral arms containing millions of stars and nebulae.

have been a cloud of hydrogen gas. At the centre, where the gas was densest, stars began to form, 'first generation' stars that have long ago died away. Some of these stars exploded as SUPERNOVAE, throwing out all the new elements such as carbon and iron.

The galaxy now has long spiral arms made up of these clouds of material and new stars. Our Sun and SOLAR SYSTEM were born in one of the arms. Every few hundred million years the Sun 'orbits' the galaxy, moving from one arm to the next. There is enough material in the arms for many generations of stars.

Millikan, Robert See Electron

Minerals

Minerals are the compounds that make up the ROCKS of the Earth. Some minerals are composed of single ELEMENTS, such as gold, copper and sulphur. Others are composed of two or more elements, such as quartz and MICA. Minerals are non-living, they are inorganic. Coal, oil and similar materials are composed of organic (once-living) matter and therefore are not minerals even though they are sometimes called minerals.

Scientists have named more than 2000 minerals, but only about 30 are common in rocks. Minerals can be

1. Solar system
2. Ring nebula
3. Orion nebula
4. Lagoon nebula
5. Triffid nebula
6. Crab nebula
7. Eagle nebula
8. Eta carinae nebula

A. Centaurus arm
B. Sagittarius arm
C. Orion arm
D. Perseus arm

▲ Four of the spiral arms of the Milky Way galaxy are named after major constellations.

▼ *Minerals vary in colour, hardness and composition. They include single elements, such as copper, gold, silver and sulphur, as well as simple and complex compounds. Some are mined for the metals they contain, such as hematite, which is an ore of iron. Malachite contains copper and is also used as an ornamental stone. Stibnite is a compound of sulphur and antimony which is found in quartz veins. Gypsum is also a sulphur compound but with calcium (calcium sulphate).*

identified by such features as colour, HARDNESS, the amount of light that can pass through them, their DENSITY and the CRYSTAL formation. The ELECTRON MICROSCOPE allows minerals to be studied in detail.

In the Earth's crust, 95 percent of the minerals are silicates, made up of different arrangements of atoms of SILICON and OXYGEN, held together by other atoms such as iron, magnesium, calcium, aluminium and potassium. Glass, brick and ceramics are mostly silicates, as are emeralds, aquamarine, topaz, agate and jasper. Decorative minerals can be polished to give gemstones.

Salt (sodium chloride) is a mineral and it is compounds such as this that are essential for complete NUTRITION along with VITAMINS.

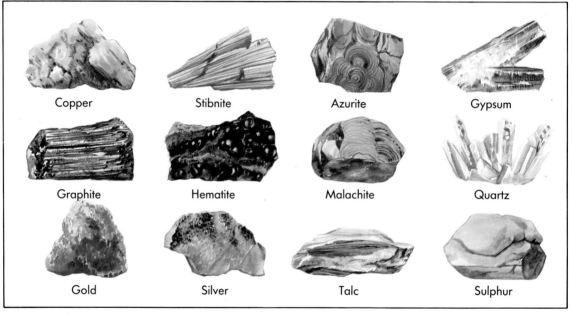

Copper   Stibnite   Azurite   Gypsum

Graphite   Hematite   Malachite   Quartz

Gold   Silver   Talc   Sulphur

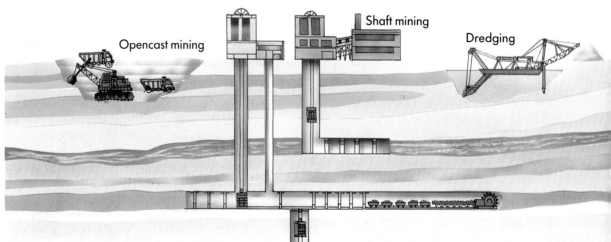

Opencast mining   Shaft mining   Dredging

◄ An aerial view of Kennecott's Bingham Canyon copper mine in Utah, United States. This large opencast mine produces much of Utah's copper.

Mining is not a new industry. Ancient Egyptian records tell of an expedition to the Sinai peninsula around 2600 BC to mine for turquoise stones. While there, the Egyptians found a much more useful mineral: copper. The ancient Greeks mined silver at Laurion, south of Athens. Some of the shafts of these mines went to a depth of 120 m.

Mining

Mining is the extraction of MATERIALS from the EARTH. Materials near the surface can be dug out by blasting with EXPLOSIVES or dragging buckets across the ground to scrape away the soil and rock in an *opencast mine*. If the material is cut out of the ground in long strips, the mine is called a *strip mine*. More commonly, mines are long shafts running deep underground following thin seams of valuable materials. Large deposits of ORES may be extracted through a network of horizontal tunnels spreading out from vertical shafts. The tunnels are extended by cutting with a large rotating drill head fitted with grinding wheels or by blasting with explosives. As material is taken out of the mine by underground conveyor belts, trains and lifts, the tunnel roofs may need to be supported by wooden beams or HYDRAULIC pit props. Materials mined include coal, diamonds and the ores of tin, iron and aluminium.

▼ There are many ways of mining, depending on the nature of the mineral deposit and its depth. Minerals that lie near the surface can be extracted by opencast mining or quarrying. Deposits on the bottom of a lake or river are removed by dredging. Drift mining and shaft mining are used to reach deeper deposits. Natural gas and oil are extracted by drilling, although some oil has to be pumped up to the surface.

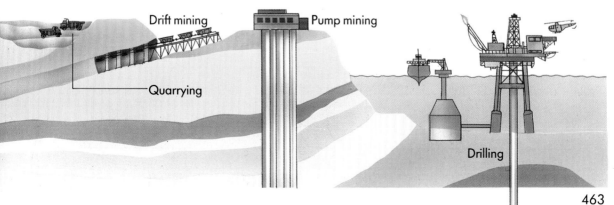

Drift mining   Pump mining

Quarrying

Drilling

▶ *A mirage is formed when rays of light are refracted, or bent, by a layer of warm air near the ground. This is why mirages are common in deserts and hot countries.*

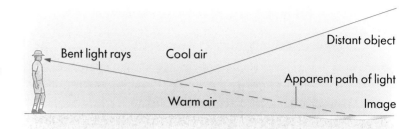

Bent light rays   Cool air   Distant object

Apparent path of light

Warm air   Image

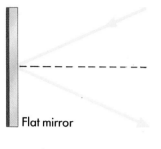

Flat mirror

Concave mirror

Convex mirror

▲ *A flat, or plane, mirror gives an undistorted image. A concave mirror, which is curved inwards like a saucer, can produce a magnified image. A convex mirror, which is curved outwards like the back of a spoon, gives a 'wide-angle' image that is reduced in size.*

▶ *A mirror which is both concave and convex gives a distorted image that makes a person look very strange.*

Mirage

Mirages are seen when LIGHT travelling through AIR follows a curved, rather than a straight, line. This happens because the air near the ground is hotter than the air higher up and expands; light then travels through it more quickly. When the light from an object reaches the eye it is travelling upwards and so appears to have come from beneath the ground. Light from the sky is also bent upwards, so there seems to be a bright patch on the ground; it looks as though the sky and the object have been reflected by a pool of water. Similar effects occur at sea, when the air is colder at sea level and warmer higher up so the light is bent downwards.

Mirror

A mirror is an object that reflects LIGHT. It is normally made from some sort of material with a smooth surface; ordinary mirrors are made from glass with a thin layer of silver on the back. A ray of light striking a flat mirror behaves like a ball striking a wall; it bounces back at the

same angle (called the *angle of reflection*) at which it made contact (the *angle of incidence*).

The surface of a *concave* mirror is curved inwards, like the bowl of a spoon. Rays of light striking a concave mirror are reflected back to a point called the FOCUS. They then spread out and form an enlarged image of the object. *Convex* mirrors, curved outwards, give a reduced image. Driving mirrors are like this. Concave mirrors are used instead of lenses to make reflecting telescopes because they produce clearer images.

Missiles

A missile is a weapon guided through the air to a target where it explodes. It is propelled through the sky by a ROCKET motor or JET ENGINE. Some missiles are directed to their targets automatically along a pre-programmed course. Others seek out a target and then lock onto it and some are guided by the person who fires them.

In an automatically guided missile, an on-board INERTIAL GUIDANCE system compares the missile's position with its pre-programmed course. If it is off-course, the guidance system moves the missile's fins to steer it back on course. Alternatively, the missile may home in on its target by locking on to the INFRARED RADIATION from the target's engines or radio energy from a RADAR aerial.

The target may be marked so that the missile recognizes it, such as by aiming an infrared beam at it. An infrared sensor in the missile steers it to the target. The person firing the missile may steer it, sending signals by

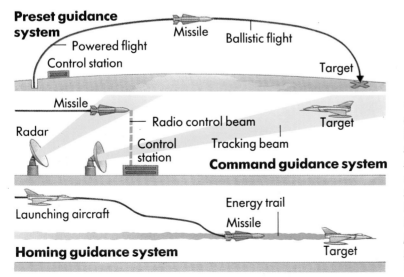

Preset guidance system

Powered flight · Missile · Ballistic flight

Control station

Target

Missile

Radar · Radio control beam · Target

Control station · Tracking beam

Command guidance system

Launching aircraft

Energy trail

Missile

Homing guidance system

Target

◀ *Guided missiles may be aimed in advance to fly to their target, using a preset guidance system. In a command guidance system, the missile obeys commands during flight which steer it to its target. Using a homing guidance system, a missile homes in on the target, perhaps by seeking the heat given out by the target's engines.*

465

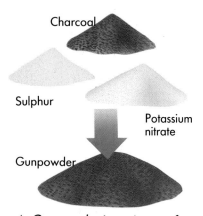

Charcoal

Sulphur

Potassium nitrate

Gunpowder

▲ *Gunpowder is a mixture of chemicals, which can be separated. But when it burns, the chemicals combine to form new compounds.*

▼ *A mixture of iron filings and sulphur can be separated using a magnet. Heating them forms the compound iron sulphide, from which the iron cannot be removed by a magnet.*

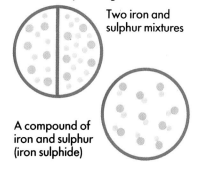

Two iron and sulphur mixtures

A compound of iron and sulphur (iron sulphide)

radio to a receiver in the missile or along a trailing wire connecting the missile to the control unit.

The missile is becoming increasingly important in modern warfare because a single well-aimed unmanned missile can destroy a ship, aircraft or tank.
See also BALLISTICS.

Mitosis *See* Cell division

Mixtures

A mixture consists of two or more substances which are not bound together chemically and so can be separated. A mixture is different from a COMPOUND, in which the substances are joined by chemical BONDS. In a mixture, the particles of each substance are distributed more or less evenly among the particles of the other substances. Powdered forms of solids put together can form mixtures. If iron filings are mixed with sand, for example, they can be separated again using a magnet.

Aerosols, COLLOIDS, EMULSIONS, foams and SOLUTIONS are all types of mixtures in which particles of one substance are scattered throughout another. The particles may be solid specks, liquid droplets or gas bubbles. The basic substances are usually liquids or gases. If the ingredients of such a mixture are evenly scattered among each other's particles, the substances are said to be *miscible*. If the particles of one stay completely separate from the particles of the other, the substances are *immiscible*. Alcohol and water are miscible. Oil and water are

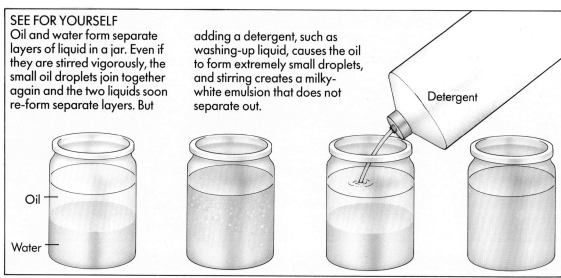

SEE FOR YOURSELF

Oil and water form separate layers of liquid in a jar. Even if they are stirred vigorously, the small oil droplets join together again and the two liquids soon re-form separate layers. But adding a detergent, such as washing-up liquid, causes the oil to form extremely small droplets, and stirring creates a milky-white emulsion that does not separate out.

Detergent

Oil

Water

immiscible. In fact, oil floats on top of water. In most mixtures, the contents will eventually separate out naturally. The ingredients of mixtures can be separated by FILTRATION, precipitation, and so on.

Modem

A modem connects a COMPUTER to other computers by TELEPHONE. The word comes from MOdulator–DEModulator. Computer data is a DIGITAL signal. Before it can be sent down a telephone line, it must be changed into an ANALOGUE form that a telephone can handle. Two notes, are used to represent a pulse and the absence of a pulse. This is called *modulation*. The notes are received by a modem at the other end and demodulated, or changed back into digital computer data.

Molecule

A molecule is the smallest particle of an ELEMENT or COMPOUND that can exist on its own. Molecules consist of two to thousands of atoms held together by chemical BONDS. A molecule of the liquid water is made up of two atoms of the gas HYDROGEN and one of the gas OXYGEN. But molecules can be more complicated than that. The bonds holding a molecule together determine its shape. For example, a molecule of ammonia, made up of one nitrogen atom and three hydrogen atoms, is pyramid-shaped. All gases and organic compounds, most liquids and many solids consist of molecules, but METALS and many compounds that form SOLUTIONS consist of IONS (atoms or groups of atoms with a positive or negative charge). Large molecules such as DNA, the genetic material, can be seen with an ELECTRON MICROSCOPE.

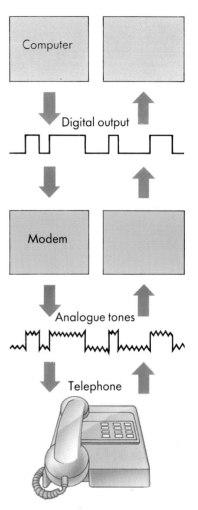

▲ A modem converts digital computer signals into analogue ones for transmission over a telephone line. At the receiver it converts analogue signals back to digital.

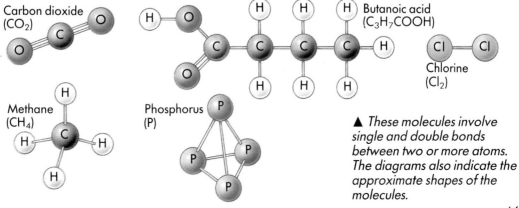

▲ These molecules involve single and double bonds between two or more atoms. The diagrams also indicate the approximate shapes of the molecules.

467

▶ *When the left-hand sphere collides with the one on its right, it passes on its momentum. This travels along the row of spheres to the one on the extreme right, which is forced to swing out.*

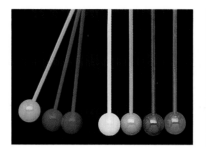
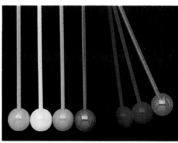

To find the **momentum** of a moving object we multiply its mass (its weight on Earth) by its velocity (its speed and direction). A car that weighs 1000 kg, driven south at a speed of 5 metres per second (m/s) has a momentum of 1000 x 5 = 5000 kg m/s towards the south. A lorry weighing 5000 kg, to have the same momentum as the car, has to be driven at only 1 m/s.

Momentum

Momentum was the name given by Newton to an object's MASS multiplied by the VELOCITY with which it is moving. If someone taps you on the shoulder with a piece of wood, you hardly feel it. But if the person swings the wood and hits you with it, the blow really hurts. The wood is not heavier, but its momentum has increased because it is moving much faster.

Because the FORCE one object exerts on another is matched by an equal and opposite force from the second object on the first, the rates at which the momenta of the two objects are changing are equal and opposite. The total momentum of the two objects does not change but is *conserved*. You can see CONSERVATION of momentum when one snooker ball strikes another so that the first ball stops dead. All its momentum has been transferred to the second ball; if the balls have the same mass, the second ball will move off with the same speed and direction as the first.

Monoclonal antibody

Antibodies are substances produced by the body in response to an antigen, which is usually the product of a harmful DISEASE. Antibodies destroy the antigen and so lessen the effect of the disease. Monoclonal antibodies

Production of monoclonal antibodies

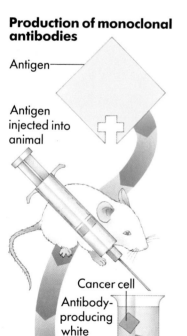

Antigen——

Antigen injected into animal

Cancer cell

Antibody-producing white blood cells from spleen

Cells combined

Cells producing antibodies isolated

Monoclonal antibody produced

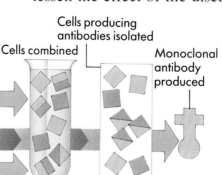

◀ *Monoclonal antibodies are produced using hybrids of white blood cells and types of cancer cells. These are cloned so that they produce pure strains of single antibodies.*

are ANTIBODIES which are produced artificially, usually by culturing, and so can be produced in large quantities and used in the treatment of many diseases. Formerly, antibodies could be given to people who were at risk of disease only by extracting them from the BLOOD of a person who had recovered from that disease. Sometimes this *serum* could be made by using the blood from animals that had been infected.

Monsoon

A monsoon describes any relatively constant WIND that tends to reverse its direction with the changing seasons. In the area around the Indian Ocean and Southern Asia, as well as around the coasts of West Africa and northern Australia, the monsoon wind blows from the north-east in the winter and from the south-west in the summer. During the summer in India the wind brings with it the heavy rains which are known as the monsoon rains or 'the rainy season'. The changing direction of the wind is brought about by regional changes in air PRESSURE which take place with the seasons.

Although the idea of a rainy season may not seem pleasant, the summer monsoon is vital to the farmers of the area because most of the annual rainfall occurs at this time and, without it, crops could not be grown.

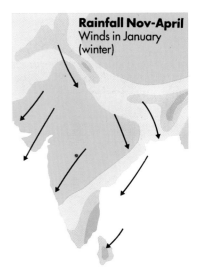

Rainfall Nov-April
Winds in January
(winter)

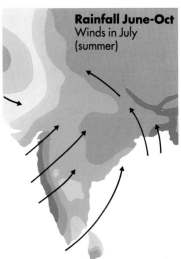

Rainfall June-Oct
Winds in July
(summer)

Centimetres
of rain

Over 175
100–175
50–100
25–50
12.5–25
2.5–12.5
Below 2.5

▲ *Monsoons are strong winds that blow in opposite directions at different times of the year. In Asia the summer monsoon, blowing off the Indian Ocean, brings a season of heavy rainfall. (Left) The rain falls so quickly that the ground is soon waterlogged.*

Moon Facts
Diameter 3476 km
Distance from Earth
384,000 km
Day length 29 d 12 h 44 min
Mass 0.012 of Earth
Density 0.61 of Earth
Surface temperature
100°C maximum
−170°C minimum

▶ The Moon is a huge ball of rock pitted with craters. Most of the craters were caused by impact from meteors, although some reveal the sites of ancient volcanoes.

SEE FOR YOURSELF
You can record the phases of the Moon by observing it on cloudless nights. It takes 28 days to pass through all the phases from New to Full and back again. Record your observations in a notebook.

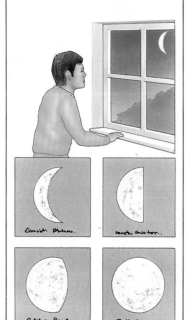

Moon

The Moon is the EARTH'S SATELLITE. It is the closest body to us, but the two bodies are completely different. Both were formed by particles colliding together some 4600 million years ago, but since the Moon is only a quarter of the Earth's diameter, it cooled down much more quickly. Its thick crust is now 'frozen' solid, while the Earth's thin crust still floats over the hot under-layers.

Soon after they formed, the Earth and the Moon probably looked similar, hot spheres being constantly cratered by impacts from rocky bodies. On the Moon the craters were preserved, with no wind or water to wear the rock away. The Earth's craters have almost all been wiped out by crust movements and weather.

The Moon has no ATMOSPHERE because its force of GRAVITY is very weak. The Moon has not been able to attract any gas molecules at all, while the Earth has held onto a dense air shield.

The Moon must once have been spinning quickly, but the Earth's pull has slowed it down so that it keeps the same face towards the Earth. Once a month, as it orbits the Earth, the Moon passes through phases from New to Full and back to New again. Sometimes we see an ECLIPSE of the Moon.

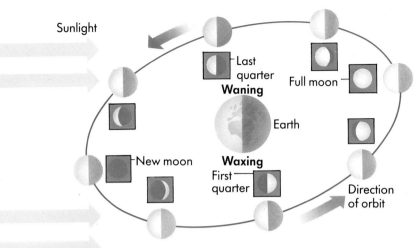

Sunlight

Last quarter
Waning
Full moon
Earth
New moon
Waxing
First quarter
Direction of orbit

◀ *Half of the Moon is always in sunlight. The phases of the Moon depend on how much of the lit half we can see from the Earth. At New Moon, when the Earth, Moon and Sun are roughly in line, we cannot see any of the lit half. About a week later, at the first quarter, we can see half of the part of the Moon that is in sunlight, and at Full Moon we can see all of it. By the last quarter we can again see only half of the lit part.*

Morgan, T. H. *See* Chromosomes and Genes

Morse, Samuel

Samuel Finley Breese Morse (1791–1872) produced a way of transmitting messages by cable using a code (Morse code). After studying art in Europe, he learned of the discovery that a pivoted magnetic needle would move if a wire carrying an electric current was brought near it. In 1832, he set out to invent a machine called a TELEGRAPH to transmit information by this method. By 1837 he was able to demonstrate a working model in New York. In 1844 a telegraph line 64 km long was set up, connecting Baltimore and Washington. Morse made an instrument in which an electric current, when turned on, worked an ELECTROMAGNET which caused a pencil to

▲ *Samuel Morse was an artist and inventor of a telegraph.*

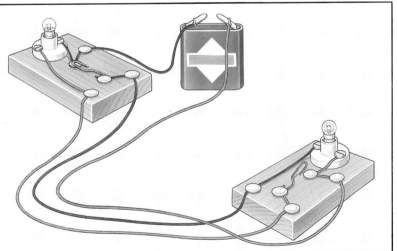

SEE FOR YOURSELF
You can make your own Morse transmitter using flashing lights. Make a pair of switches using drawing pins and paper clips. Connect the switches to a battery and lamp holders as shown, and connect the two lamp holders together with long lengths of wire. The two operators can be in different rooms. Send messages in Morse code using long and short flashes of light to represent dashes and dots.

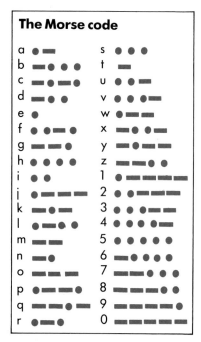

The Morse code

a	•▬	s	•••
b	▬•••	t	▬
c	▬•▬•	u	••▬
d	▬••	v	•••▬
e	•	w	•▬▬
f	••▬•	x	▬••▬
g	▬▬•	y	▬•▬▬
h	••••	z	▬▬••
i	••	1	•▬▬▬▬
j	•▬▬▬	2	••▬▬▬
k	▬•▬	3	•••▬▬
l	•▬••	4	••••▬
m	▬▬	5	•••••
n	▬•	6	▬••••
o	▬▬▬	7	▬▬•••
p	•▬▬•	8	▬▬▬••
q	▬▬•▬	9	▬▬▬▬•
r	•▬•	0	▬▬▬▬▬

▲ *The Morse code uses dots and dashes to stand for the letters and numbers.*

▶ *In a simple direct current electric motor, current from a battery flows through a coil of wire. The coil is pivoted in the magnetic field between the poles of a magnet, which makes the wire move so that the coil rotates. Brushes keep the current flowing in the same direction.*

Mountain Heights
The 10 highest mountains in the world are all over 8000 m and they all form part of the Himalayas on the borders of Nepal with India and Tibet.
Everest 8848 m
Godwin Austen 8611 m
Kanchenjunga 8598 m
Lhotse I 8501 m
Makalu 8481 m
Lhotse II 8383 m
Dhaulagiri 8172 m
Cho Oyu 8153 m
Manaslu 8125 m
Annapurna 8078 m

mark a moving strip of paper. The current was repeatedly turned on and off by a tapping key and information was sent in the form of on-off pulses, the code.
See also COMMUNICATIONS; DIGITAL.

Morton, William *See* Pain

Motion *See* Movement and Motion

Motor, electric

An electric motor is a MACHINE that converts electrical ENERGY into movement. It relies on the fact that a wire carrying an electric current moves in a magnetic field. There are electric motors in refrigerators, hair-dryers, food processors, clocks and many other objects.

In most motors the magnet stands still, while the coil of wire carrying the current moves inside it. When a current flows through the coil, the coil becomes a magnet, with a north and a south pole. Since unlike poles attract and like poles repel, the coil swings round between the

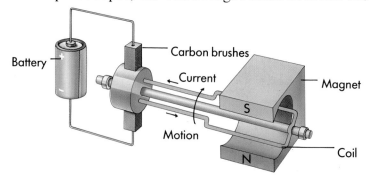

poles of the fixed magnet until its north pole is facing the south pole of the magnet and its south pole is facing the magnet's north pole. The direction of the current in the coil is therefore reversed so that the coil's poles are reversed. The coil swings round again half a turn to line up its poles once more. As the current keeps being reversed, the coil keeps turning. If the current supply to the coil is direct (d.c.), a commutator is needed to keep reversing the current.
See also GENERATOR; INDUCTANCE.

Mountains

A mountain is an area of high ground which usually rises steeply to a summit. Most mountains are formed by a

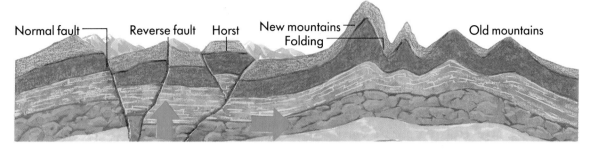

Normal fault   Reverse fault   Horst   New mountains / Folding   Old mountains

▲ *Mountains are formed by faults and folding of the Earth's crust. New mountains are tall and jagged. Old mountains are more rounded because they have been worn down by weathering and erosion.*

◄ *The Andes form a chain of mountains that run down the western side of South America. Many of them are volcanoes.*

process known as 'mountain building' caused by the mechanisms of PLATE TECTONICS. The interior of the EARTH is constantly on the move, affecting the thin, solid crust on which we all live. Large amounts of sediment are deposited in a subsiding area of the sea. Later the processes of folding and faulting, associated with earthquake and volcanic activity at a plate margin, cause the sediments to be thrust upwards as rocky mountains. Mountains' origins can be shown because the fossil remains of sea creatures have been found in the rocks hundreds of metres above sea level.

Consider three mountain ranges: those of Scotland (the Caledonian mountains); the Alps; and the Himalayas. The mountains of Scotland are old and have undergone some 500 million years of EROSION AND WEATHERING while the Alps and Himalayas are progressively younger and have had less time to be worn away and so are much higher.

1
2
3 Tree line
4
5

1 Snow cap
2 Alpine plants
3 Pasture
4 Coniferous trees
5 Deciduous trees

Movement and Motion

Motion occurs when something changes its position. Even plants move, though their ROOTS remain in the same place. Almost all animals can move, some further than others. Humans can not only move but have invented objects that can move. *See* pages 474 and 475.

▲ *The kinds of plants that grow on a mountain vary with the altitude. Below the tree line, the chief plants are trees. Above that line, the only plants are small ones that have adapted to growing in the low temperatures.*

MOVEMENT AND MOTION

Everything in the Universe is in motion. The Earth moves round the Sun and the Solar System is moving in relation to the galaxy. The rate of motion is called the speed and it is measured by calculating the distance moved in a certain time. Objects that are accelerating are increasing their speed. The velocity of an object describes its speed and its direction. A vehicle, or an animal, moving around a corner at a constant speed has a changing velocity. Machines can be made to move by a variety of means. They are supplied with energy which is converted into movement.

It is important for animals to be able to move about, to find food and mates, and to escape from their enemies, although some aquatic creatures remain in one place and sift their food from the passing water. These creatures are usually protected by shells. Most animals run, crawl, swim or fly with the aid of limbs. The limbs are moved by muscles, which are attached to the skeleton. When the muscles contract they move the skeleton, and with it part or all of the body. The cheetah's powerful leg muscles allow the animal to reach speeds of over 100 km/h for short distances. Animals without any hard skeleton, such as earthworms, rely on hydraulic mechanisms to produce movement. Their muscles act on the fluids in their bodies and, because fluids cannot be compressed, the body changes shape and moves. For example, when the circular muscles running around an earthworm's body contract and squeeze the body the worm becomes long and thin. When the muscles running along the body contract it becomes shorter, but the fluid has to go somewhere and so the worm becomes fat. The earthworm moves by alternately stretching and contracting its body.

▲ Every moving object has kinetic energy, which depends on the object's mass and how fast it is moving. A moving object can transfer kinetic energy to a stationary one.

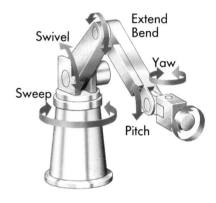

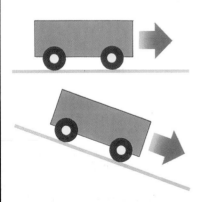

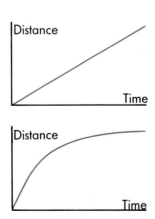

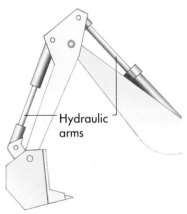

▲ Machines can carry out many different types of movements. The robot arm (top) can carry out combinations of movements that put the 'hand' into any position that is required. The hydraulic digger arm (bottom) can only move forwards and backwards.

For a space rocket to escape from the Earth's gravity it has to reach the phenomenal speed of just over 11 km/s (more than 40,000 km/h).

▲ The speed of an object is the distance it travels in a certain time. On the graph a constant speed is a straight line. (Below) If the rate of change of distance with time changes, the object is accelerating.

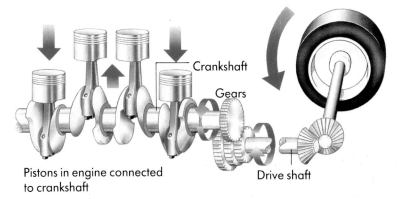

Crankshaft

Gears

Pistons in engine connected to crankshaft

Drive shaft

◄ *Cranks and gears change the direction and speed of motion. In a car or other road vehicle, cranks convert the up-and-down motion of the pistons in the engine into the rotary motion of the drive shaft. A set of gears allows the shaft to turn at different speeds. A pair of bevel gears makes the drive shaft turn the axle and with it the vehicle's wheels.*

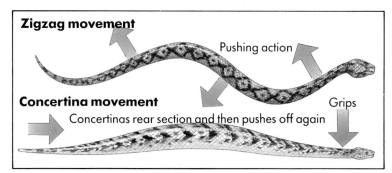

Zigzag movement

Pushing action

Concertina movement

Concertinas rear section and then pushes off again

Grips

◄ *A snake moves by forming its body into a zig-zag, gripping the ground with its undersides and pushing itself forwards.*

▼ *A fish swims by flexing its body and tail fins from side to side. It does this by alternately contracting muscles on each side of its body. As one set of muscles contract the muscles on the other side (sometimes known as the opposing muscles) are stretched to relax them and allow the body to retain its shape.*

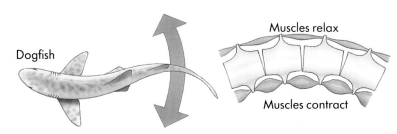

Dogfish

Muscles relax

Muscles contract

Muscles contract

Muscles relax

SEE FOR YOURSELF
Plants can move too. They move when they grow towards the light, also their stems grow upwards and their roots grow down. You can see this by taking a pot plant and putting it on its side. Its horizontal stem will bend and gradually turn upward.

▲ *A frog leaps powerfully out of the water to make a meal of an unsuspecting insect. Many predators rely on speed to catch their prey.*

See also ACCELERATION; ENERGY; ENGINE; GEARS; HYDRAULICS; MASS; MECHANICS; MUSCLES; ORBIT; SKELETON; UNIVERSE; VELOCITY.

Andreas Vesalius (1514–1564)
Vesalius was a Flemish doctor who was the first to disagree with the teachings of the Ancient Greek physician Galen, whose ideas about the workings of the human body had remained unchallenged for 1300 years. Galen was a thinker. But Vesalius was a practical scientist who dissected dead bodies to find out how human anatomy works, from the muscles and bones to the internal organs.

Multimedia

Multimedia is a joining together of text, graphics, photographs, and moving pictures held in a CD-ROM drive in a computer. Some multimedia systems such as CD-I (Compact Disc Interactive) operate with a TV set. Multimedia programs are increasingly used in education, entertainment and other areas, and personal computers allow users to take an active part in the program.

CD-ROMs are used and made in much the same way as audio compact disc players. They are essential in multimedia programs because they can hold a very large amount of data — hundreds of megabytes — and this is constantly being increased. Many more bytes are needed to record sound or pictures than are needed for the printed word.

Muscle

All animal movements are controlled by muscles, which work by pulling against the SKELETON. Muscles are made of bundles of fibres, which shorten when they receive a signal from the NERVES. The power of a muscle depends on the number of fibres. These increase with exercise, which is why body builders develop big muscles.

There are three types of muscles. In humans, voluntary muscles produce most movements. As they shorten, they pull against the bone to which they are fastened, causing it to move. These muscles are usually found in pairs, which can pull in opposite directions. They are said to be antagonistic. A few muscles are attached to the skin, and on the head and face these are responsible for facial expressions.

Smooth or involuntary muscles work automatically to keep the body systems operating properly, for example, the intestines. The third type of muscle is cardiac muscle, which causes the heart to pump. This type of muscle works throughout life. It continues to pump even when it is disconnected from the nervous system, as happens in transplanted hearts.

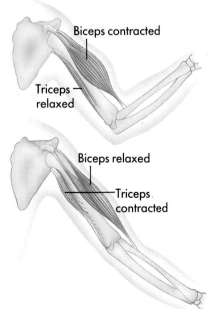

◄ *Movement of a limb, such as the forearm, requires the combined action of a pair of muscles. When the biceps muscle in the upper arm contracts, the arm bends at the elbow. To straighten the arm again, the triceps muscle at the back of the arm contracts causing the biceps to relax.*